Real MOM Kitchen

Real MOM Kitchen

KEEPIN' IT REAL IN THE KITCHEN

LAURA POWELL

FRONT TABLE BOOKS
SPRINGVILLE, UTAH

ISBN 13: 978-1-59955-482-2

Published by Front Table Books, an imprint of Cedar Fort, Inc., 2373 W. 700 S., Springville, UT 84663
Distributed by Cedar Fort, Inc., www.cedarfort.com

LIBRARY OF CONGRESS CATALOGING-IN-PUBLICATION DATA

Powell, Laura (Laura Whittemore), 1974- , author.
  Real mom kitchen cookbook / Laura Powell.
      p. cm.
  Includes bibliographical references and index.
  ISBN 978-1-59955-482-2 (alk. paper)
  1. Cooking, American. I. Title.
  TX715.P8775 2011
  641.5973--dc22
                              2010051253

Cover and page design by Danie Romrell
Cover design © 2011 by Lyle Mortimer
Edited by Kelley Konzak

Printed in China

10 9 8 7 6 5 4 3 2 1

Printed on acid-free paper

Special thanks to my husband and mom, who have helped make this book possible by supporting me and being my editors.
This book is dedicated to my cute family, who taste-tests all of the recipes, and to my readers at RealMomKitchen.com who helped bring me to this place.

Table of Contents

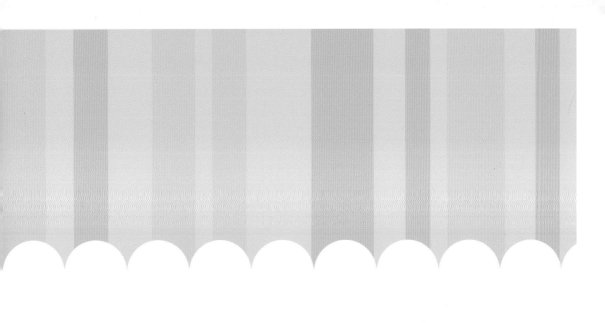

APPETIZERS AND SIDES

Cheese Potatoes

THESE POTATOES ARE A BIG HIT AT OUR HOUSE AND ARE REQUESTED OFTEN BY THE KIDS. WHO DOESN'T LOVE POTATOES DRENCHED IN CHEESE?

8–10 medium potatoes

1 small onion, diced

¼ cup butter

2 (10¾-oz.) cans cream of chicken soup

1 cup sour cream

2 cups cheddar cheese, grated

1 Preheat oven to 350 degrees.

2 Peel potatoes and place in a large saucepan. Cover with water and boil until tender, 15–20 minutes.

3 In another pan, cook onion in butter until tender. Drain potatoes and cut into small pieces.

4 In a large bowl, mix potatoes, onion, and butter with soup, sour cream, and cheese. Pour into 9×13 baking dish. Cover with foil and bake for 1 hour at 350 degrees.

Serves 8–10.

My Aunt's Potato Casserole

THIS IS ANOTHER YUMMY WAY TO EAT POTATOES. THIS DISH IS COMMONLY REFERRED TO AS FUNERAL POTATOES IN UTAH BECAUSE IT IS OFTEN SERVED ALONG WITH HAM AT LUNCHEONS FOLLOWING A FUNERAL.

1 (32-oz.) pkg. shredded hash browns, thawed

2 (10¾-oz.) cans condensed cream of mushroom soup

2 cups sour cream

½ cup butter, melted

1 cup cheddar cheese, shredded

¼ cup green onion, diced

   pepper (optional)

Topping:

2 cups cornflakes, lightly crushed

¼ cup butter, melted

1 Preheat oven to 350 degrees.

2 Combine hash browns, soup, sour cream, butter, cheddar cheese, and green onion in a large bowl. Mix well. You can add a little pepper if desired.

3 Pour hash browns mixture into 9×13 baking dish. Mix together topping ingredients and sprinkle over the hash browns mixture. Bake at 350 degrees, uncovered, for about 40 minutes until bubbly and golden.

Serves 8–10.

Lemon Cheesecake Fruit Dip

LEMON ADDS SUCH FRESHNESS TO ANY DISH. AND WHO WOULDN'T LOVE TO EAT FRESH FRUIT WITH A DIP THAT TASTES LIKE CHEESECAKE?

1 (6-oz.) container lemon flavored yogurt

1 (7-oz.) container marshmallow cream

1 (8-oz.) container whipped cream cheese

zest of 1 lemon

1 With a hand mixer, blend all ingredients into a medium-size bowl until smooth.

2 Serve with fresh fruit.

Makes about 2½ cups.

Friendship Dip

YOUR FRIENDS WILL DEFINITELY THANK YOU FOR SERVING THEM THIS YUMMY WARM DIP. IT IS TOO GOOD NOT TO SHARE WITH OTHERS.

1 (8-oz.) pkg. cream cheese, softened

1 (15-oz.) can chili

1 (4-oz.) can diced green chilies

cheddar cheese, shredded

olives, sliced

green onion (optional)

1 Preheat oven to 350 degrees.

2 Spread cream cheese evenly to cover the bottom of a pie plate.

3 Layer the following on top of cream cheese in this order: chili, green chilies, shredded cheddar cheese (enough to cover), and sliced olives.

4 Bake at 350 degrees, uncovered, until hot and melted (20–25 minutes).

5 Garnish with green onion and serve with your favorite tortilla chips.

Serves 6–8.

Taco Bean Chip Dip

MY MOM WOULD MAKE THIS WARM BEAN DIP EACH YEAR AROUND THE HOLIDAY SEASON. WATCH HOW FAST THIS DIP DISAPPEARS.

1 lb. hamburger

½ onion, diced

2 (8-oz.) cans tomato sauce

1 pkg. taco seasoning

2 (16-oz.) cans refried beans

1 (8-oz.) bottle taco sauce

3 cups cheddar cheese, shredded

sour cream

olives, sliced

1 In a large skillet, brown hamburger and onion until hamburger is no longer pink; drain.

2 Add tomato sauce and taco seasoning to meat and let simmer for a few minutes.

3 Stir in refried beans, taco sauce, and cheese.

4 Pour mixture into a 7×11 or 2-quart baking dish and bake at 400 degrees, uncovered, for 25 minutes.

5 Remove from oven and allow to cool slightly.

6 Decorate with sour cream and olives.

7 Serve with your favorite tortilla chips.

Makes 8 cups.

Mom's Sage Dressing

MY MOM LEARNED HOW TO MAKE THIS SIMPLE AND DELICIOUS DRESSING FROM MY DAD'S MOTHER. IT'S ALWAYS ON THE TABLE FOR THANKSGIVING.

2 loaves sandwich bread

2–3 tsp. ground sage

4 stalks celery, finely diced

2 medium onions, finely diced

4 Tbsp. butter

1 Preheat oven to 350 degrees.

2 Slice loaves of bread into small cubes. Place in a large pot or on a cookie sheet. Sprinkle with sage and toss bread. You want each piece of bread to get a little sprinkling of sage. Use more sage if needed.

3 Place diced celery in a sauté pan with just enough water to cover. Cook over medium heat until tender.

4 Add celery along with water to bread and toss.

5 Sauté onion in butter over medium heat until translucent. Toss in with the bread mixture.

6 At this point, you want the bread to be just slightly moist and sticky. If needed, add more water to get it to this consistency.

7 Place bread mixture in a pocket made of foil (wrapped tight). Bake at 350 degrees for 30 minutes.

Serves 20.

Cheesy Broccoli Casserole

THIS IS ONE WAY I CAN GET MY KIDS TO EAT THEIR VEGGIES. THE BROCCOLI CAN BE
SUBSTITUTED WITH A BROCCOLI, CAULIFLOWER, AND CARROT BLEND.

1 (16-oz.) bag frozen broccoli

¼ cup butter

4 oz. Velveeta® cheese

1 sleeve Ritz® crackers

⅓ cup butter, melted

1 Preheat oven to 350 degrees.

2 Cook broccoli according to package directions.
Drain and arrange in a 9×9 baking dish.

3 In a saucepan, melt ¼ cup butter and Velveeta®
together until combined. Pour over broccoli.

4 Crush sleeve of crackers, mix with ⅓ cup melted
butter, and pour on top of cheese and broccoli.

5 Bake at 350 degrees, uncovered, for 30 minutes.

Serves 6–8.

Yorkshire Pudding

MAKE THIS YORKSHIRE PUDDING IN PLACE OF MASHED POTATOES THE NEXT TIME YOU MAKE A BEEF ROAST. THESE LITTLE PUDDINGS ARE THE PERFECT ACCOMPANIMENT AND ARE DELICIOUS TOPPED WITH BEEF GRAVY.

1 cup flour

½ tsp. salt

2 eggs

½–¾ cup water

½ cup milk

2 Tbsp. vegetable or canola oil

1 Preheat oven to 425 degrees.

2 In a medium bowl, combine flour, salt, eggs, water, and milk to make thick, gravy-like batter.

3 Let the batter rest for 1 hour if you have the time, but this isn't necessary. Resting makes the pudding lighter.

4 In a 12-count muffin tin, put ½ teaspoon vegetable or canola oil in the bottom of each muffin cup.

5 Divide batter among muffin cups and bake at 425 for 20 minutes (or 350 degrees for 30–40 minutes) until puffy and golden brown.

6 Serve topped with beef gravy.

Makes 12.

Crock-Pot® Pineapple Baked Beans

THIS RECIPE COMES FROM MY MOTHER-IN-LAW. I LOVE THE SWEETNESS THAT THE PINEAPPLE ADDS. PLUS, I LOVE THAT IT CAN BE MADE IN THE CROCK-POT® AND SERVED NICE AND WARM.

1 lb. bacon, diced

1 onion, diced

1 green pepper, diced

2 (31-oz.) cans pork and beans

1 (20-oz.) can crushed pineapple, drained

1 cup brown sugar

1 (16-oz.) bottle ketchup

6 Tbsp. Worcestershire sauce

1 In a large skillet, cook bacon until halfway cooked.

2 Add onion and green pepper.

3 Continue to cook until bacon is crisp and onion and green pepper are softened. Drain.

4 In a 3-quart Crock-Pot®, blend together pork and beans, pineapple, brown sugar, ketchup, and Worcestershire sauce.

5 Add bacon mixture to beans and stir to combine. Cook on low for 3 hours.

Serves 12.

Fresh Fruit Dip

THIS FRUIT DIP IS A FAVORITE OF MINE. I LOVE THE FLAVOR YOU GET FROM THE ORANGE AND THE SLIGHT TANG FROM THE SOUR CREAM.

1 cup milk

1 (3.3-oz.) pkg. instant vanilla pudding mix

½ of a 12-oz. can frozen orange juice concentrate

1 cup sour cream

1 In a blender, combine milk, pudding mix, and frozen orange juice concentrate.

2 Blend well.

3 Pour into a bowl and whisk in sour cream until smooth.

4 Serve with fresh fruit.

Makes about 2 cups.

Crock-Pot Refried Beans

THESE BEANS ARE BETTER THAN WHAT YOU WILL FIND IN A CAN. THEY ARE PERFECT FOR USING IN ANY DISH BUT ARE ALSO GREAT FOR DIPPING TORTILLA CHIPS.

3 cups dry pinto beans, rinsed

1 onion, diced

9 cups water

5 tsp. salt

1¾ tsp. pepper

2 Tbsp. minced garlic

⅛ tsp. ground cumin

1 Combine all ingredients in a Crock-Pot® and stir until well combined.

2 Set Crock-Pot® to high and cook for 8 hours.

3 Drain and reserve the liquid.

4 Mash beans using a potato masher or a fork.

5 Mix in some of the reserved liquid, a bit at a time, until the mixture reaches the desired consistency. Add enough liquid to make the beans slightly runnier than you want because the mixture will thicken as it sits.

Makes about 6 cups.

Crab Spread

THIS RECIPE COMES FROM MY MOM. IT WAS SERVED OFTEN AT PROGRESSIVE DINNERS WE WOULD HAVE WITH FAMILY DURING THE HOLIDAYS.

1 (6-oz.) pkg. frozen imitation crab, thawed

1 (8-oz.) pkg. cream cheese, softened

2 Tbsp. lemon juice

2 green onions, finely chopped

   dash of salt

   dash of pepper

   dash of garlic salt

1 Flake thawed imitation crab and set aside.

2 In a bowl, combine remaining ingredients until smooth and creamy.

3 Fold in imitation crab.

4 Serve on your favorite crackers.

Makes 1½ cups.

Shrimp Dip

THIS DIP IS A RECIPE THAT COMES FROM MY GRANDMA. IT COULD BE FOUND ON THE TABLE AT ALMOST EVERY FAMILY GATHERING AT HER HOME.

1 (8-oz.) pkg. cream cheese, softened

2 celery leaves, chopped

2 green onions, diced

   dash of garlic salt

   pepper to taste

1 (6.5-oz.) can shrimp, drained

   milk

1 In a bowl, combine the cream cheese, celery leaves, green onion, garlic salt, pepper, and shrimp with a hand mixer until well blended.

2 Add a small amount of milk and blend until the dip is the consistency of a chip dip.

Makes about 1½ cups.

Clam Dip

THIS IS A FAVORITE RECIPE MY MOM MAKES FREQUENTLY. YOU CAN OFTEN FIND IT PILED ON PLATES AT FAMILY GATHERINGS AND DEVOURED WITH SALTY POTATO CHIPS. EVEN MY HUSBAND, WHO ISN'T A SEAFOOD FAN, LOVES THIS DIP.

1 (6.5-oz.) can minced clams

2 (8-oz.) pkgs. cream cheese

3 squirts of lemon juice

3 squirts of Worcestershire sauce

1 heaping Tbsp. mayonnaise

salt and pepper to taste

milk

1 In a bowl, combine clams, cream cheese, lemon juice, Worcestershire sauce, mayonnaise, season salt, and pepper with a hand mixer until well combined.

2 Mix in enough milk to make consistency of chip dip.

Makes about 2½ cups.

Vegetable Dip

IF I AM GOING TO EAT RAW VEGGIES, THIS IS MY FAVORITE WAY TO EAT THEM;
ACCOMPANIED BY THIS CREAMY AND FLAVORFUL VEGETABLE DIP.

1 cup sour cream

1 cup mayonnaise

2 tsp. dried onion

2 tsp. Bon Appetit or Beau Monde seasoning

2 tsp. dill weed

1 In a bowl, mix all ingredients until well combined.

2 Cover and refrigerate for at least 2 hours to blend flavors.

3 Serve with raw cut vegetables. Also works well for chips.

Makes 2 cups.

Black Bean and Corn Salsa

MY FAMILY CAN OFTEN BE FOUND IN THE SUMMER SITTING AROUND A BIG BOWL OF THIS DIP. IT IS THE PERFECT DIP FOR PARTIES OR FOR JUST HANGING OUT ON THE BACK PORCH.

1 (15-oz.) can corn, drained

1 (15-oz.) can black beans, rinsed and drained

1 (10-oz.) can diced tomatoes with green chilies

½–1 cup prepared Italian dressing

½ Tbsp. lime juice

½ tsp. chili powder

1 Combine corn, black beans, and diced tomatoes in a medium bowl.

2 Add prepared Italian dressing, using enough to cover all of the bean mixture.

3 Add lime juice and chili powder and mix well.

4 Chill salsa in the refrigerator for at least 1 hour, but 12–24 hours is best.

5 When ready to serve, drain salsa in a colander to remove excess liquid.

6 Serve with your favorite tortilla chips.

Makes about 6 cups.

Fried Wontons

I LOVE A GOOD WONTON, AND THIS RECIPE IS FABULOUS. THE FILLING IS FULL OF FLAVOR, AND I LOVE TO SERVE THEM WITH PREPARED SWEET AND SOUR SAUCE.

2 cups cooked chicken, diced

½ cup celery, chopped

¼ cup green onion, chopped

1 (4-oz.) can diced green chilies

2 Tbsp. chili sauce

1 egg

1 (12-oz.) pkg. square wonton wrappers

1 In a medium bowl, mix chicken, celery, onion, chilies, and chili sauce together.

2 In a small bowl, beat egg.

3 Wet 2 adjacent edges of each wonton wrapper with egg.

4 Place 1 teaspoon of filling mixture in the wonton.

5 Fold wonton over from one corner to the other so that the 2 dry edges meet the 2 wet edges and it looks like a triangle.

6 Fry both sides in hot oil until golden crisp. Drain on paper towel.

7 Serve with your favorite sweet and sour sauce.

Serves 6.

Cottage Cheese Ranch Crackers

COTTAGE CHEESE—TOPPED CRACKERS ARE A FAVORITE SNACK OF MINE. THIS RECIPE HELPS GIVE THE COTTAGE CHEESE EXTRA FLAVOR.

1 (24-oz.) container small curd cottage cheese

2 cups sour cream

1 ranch party dip mix

   buttery crackers (such as Ritz®, Club®, or Town House® crackers)

1 Mix first 3 ingredients together in a bowl and chill for at least 1 hour.

2 Serve mixture on top of crackers. Also works well as a vegetable dip.

Makes 5 cups.

BREADS

Divine Breadsticks

THIS IS MY GO-TO BREADSTICK RECIPE. IT'S MADE FROM SCRATCH BUT COMES TOGETHER IN AN HOUR.

1½   cups warm water

1   Tbsp. yeast

2   Tbsp. sugar

3½   cups flour

½   tsp. salt

6   Tbsp. butter

1   tsp. garlic salt

Parmesan cheese

1 Preheat oven to 375 degrees.

2 In the bowl of a stand mixer, combine water, yeast, sugar, flour, and salt. Using the dough hook attachment, knead together for three minutes. Let dough rest for 10 minutes.

3 In a small saucepan, melt butter and mix in garlic salt.

4 Roll dough out into a 9×13 rectangle. Using a pizza cutter, cut dough into 12 strips.

5 Roll each strip in butter mixture, twist dough, and place on a large baking sheet.

6 Sprinkle with Parmesan cheese. Cover breadsticks and let rise 30 minutes.

7 Bake at 375 degrees for 15–20 minutes until golden brown.

Makes 12 breadsticks.

Easy Peasant Bread

THIS REALLY SHOULD BE CALLED "BREAD RECIPE FOR DUMMIES." IT IS HARD TO MESS THIS ONE UP. THIS BREAD HAS A VERY RUSTIC LOOK TO IT. IF YEAST BREAD SCARES YOU, GIVE THIS ONE A TRY.

1 pkg. dry yeast

2 cups warm water

1 Tbsp. sugar

2 tsp. salt

4 cups flour

   cornmeal

   melted butter

1 Place yeast, water, sugar, and salt in a large bowl and stir until dissolved.

2 Add flour and stir until well blended. Do not knead. Cover and let rise until double in size (about 1 hour).

3 Remove dough from bowl and place in 2 rounds on a greased cookie sheet sprinkled with cornmeal. Let rise an additional hour.

4 Brush top of dough with melted butter and bake in preheated oven at 425 degrees for 10 minutes.

5 Reduce oven temperature to 375 degrees and cook for an additional 15 minutes.

6 Serve warm.

Makes 2 loaves.

30-Minute Rolls

YES, YOU CAN MAKE HOMEMADE ROLLS IN 30 MINUTES. IT IS ALL POSSIBLE WITH THIS RECIPE.

1 cup + 2 Tbsp. warm water

⅓ cup oil

2 Tbsp. yeast

¼ cup sugar

½ tsp. salt

1 egg

3½ cups flour

1 Preheat oven to 400 degrees.

2 In the bowl of a stand mixer, combine water, oil, yeast, and sugar. Allow mixture to rest for 15 minutes.

3 With a dough hook, mix in salt, egg, and 2 cups of flour until combined. Add remaining flour ½ cup at a time.

4 Shape dough into 12 balls and let rest for 10 minutes.

5 Place rolls in a greased 9x13 pan or baking sheet. Bake at 400 degrees for 10 minutes until tops are golden brown.

Makes 12 rolls.

Five Star Corn Bread

THIS IS MY FAVORITE CORN BREAD RECIPE. IT'S ALMOST AS EASY AS MAKING IT FROM A MIX. I LOVE TO SERVE IT WITH HONEY BUTTER.

3   eggs

1½ cups milk

3   cups baking mix

3   heaping Tbsp. cornmeal

1   cup melted butter (no substitutes)

¾   tsp. baking powder

1   cup sugar

1 Preheat oven to 350 degrees.

2 Mix all ingredients in a bowl with fork (not a mixer, or it will fall). Mixture will have small lumps.

3 Pour batter into an ungreased 9×13 pan.

4 Bake at 350 degrees for 40–45 minutes.

5 Serve while warm with honey butter.

Serves 12–15.

Mom's Orange Rolls

THIS RECIPE IS ONE OF MY ABSOLUTE, ALL-TIME FAVORITE ROLL RECIPES. THIS RECIPE COMES FROM MY MOM, AND SHE'S BEEN MAKING THEM AS LONG AS I CAN REMEMBER. THESE ROLLS OFTEN MAKE IT TO THE THANKSGIVING DINNER TABLE. THE DOUGH IS MADE THE NIGHT BEFORE AND KEPT IN THE FRIDGE.

½   cup warm water

2   pkgs. yeast

½   cup margarine or butter

½   cup sugar

1   cup hot water

2   tsp. salt

3   eggs, well beaten

4–4½ cups flour

Filling:

½   cup butter, melted

½   cup sugar

    zest of 1 orange

Frosting:

2   cups powdered sugar

4–6 Tbsp. fresh orange juice

1 In a large bowl, combine water and yeast and let sit.

2 Melt butter in a saucepan and mix in sugar and hot water.

3 Combine butter mixture with yeast mixture. Then add in eggs and flour until well combined.

4 Cover bowl and let dough sit in the refrigerator overnight.

5 Divide dough into two balls. Roll each ball out into a 9x13-inch rectangle on a lightly floured surface.

6 Mix together filling ingredients and spread mixture over both rectangles.

7 Roll up dough from one long side to the other long side.

8 Cut each roll into 12 pieces and place in greased muffin tins.

9 Let rise 3 to 4 hours.

10 Bake in preheated oven at 375 degrees for 10–12 minutes until golden brown. Allow to cool slightly.

11 In a small bowl, mix together frosting ingredients and spread on top of warm rolls.

Makes 24 rolls.

Pumpkin Chocolate Chip Bread

I LOVE THE TASTE OF PUMPKIN WITH CHOCOLATE. EVERY TIME FALL ROLLS AROUND, YOU CAN FIND THIS BREAD IN MY HOUSE.

1 (29-oz.) can pumpkin

4½ cups flour

1½ tsp. salt

1½ tsp. nutmeg

1½ tsp. cloves

5 eggs

1½ tsp. soda

4½ tsp. cinnamon

1 tsp. ginger

3½ cups sugar

2 cups oil

1 cup chocolate chips

1 Preheat oven to 350 degrees.

2 In a large bowl, mix together all ingredients except chocolate chips until just combined.

3 Fold in chips.

4 Divide mixture between 2 well-greased loaf pans and bake at 350 degrees for 1 hour or until toothpick inserted in center of loaf comes out clean.

Makes 2 loaves.

Overnight Cran-Orange Pull-Aparts

I MAKE THIS RECIPE EACH YEAR FOR CHRISTMAS MORNING. IT'S PERFECT BECAUSE I PUT IT TOGETHER THE NIGHT BEFORE. THEN WHEN I GET UP IN THE MORNING, IT'S ALL READY TO PUT IN THE OVEN WHILE WE OPEN PRESENTS. I LOVE TO SERVE IT WITH A GLASS OF MILK, JUICE, OR HOT CHOCOLATE.

¼ cup dried cranberries

16 frozen white dough rolls (still frozen)

¼ cup sugar

1 (3.4-oz.) pkg. vanilla instant pudding mix

zest of 1 orange

½ cup butter, melted

Frosting:

1 cup powdered sugar

1 Tbsp. butter, melted

2 Tbsp. fresh orange juice

1 Sprinkle cranberries in the bottom of a greased bundt pan.

2 Arrange rolls evenly in the pan.

3 Mix sugar and dry pudding together and sprinkle over rolls.

4 Combine orange rind with melted butter and spoon over rolls.

5 Cover pan with plastic wrap that has been sprayed with non-stick cooking spray. Place pan in cold oven overnight (8–10 hours).

6 Remove pan from oven.

7 Preheat oven to 350 degrees. Remove plastic wrap from pan and bake for 25 minutes.

8 Immediately invert pan onto a serving platter.

9 Cool slightly. Combine frosting ingredients together and drizzle over pull-aparts.

Serves 24.

Easy Parmesan Knots

THESE ROLLS COME TOGETHER IN A JIFFY THANKS TO REFRIGERATED BISCUIT DOUGH. THEY ARE PERFECT TO ACCOMPANY A BOWL OF SOUP OR A PLATE OF PASTA.

1 (12-oz.) tube refrigerated buttermilk biscuits

¼ cup canola oil

3 Tbsp. Parmesan cheese, grated

½ tsp. garlic powder

1 tsp. dried oregano

1 tsp. dried parsley flakes

1 Preheat oven to 400 degrees.

2 On a lightly floured surface, roll each biscuit into a 12-inch rope and tie into a knot, tucking ends under.

3 Place on a large greased baking sheet.

4 Bake at 400 degrees for 8–10 minutes until golden brown.

5 Mix together remaining ingredients and brush on knots.

Makes 8.

Two-Way Zucchini Bread

ONE WAY I CAN GET MY FAMILY TO EAT ZUCCHINI IS IN THIS BREAD. THE GREAT THING IS, YOU CAN MAKE IT TWO WAYS—REGULAR OR CHOCOLATE.

2 cups white sugar

1 cup vegetable oil

3 eggs

3 tsp. vanilla extract

2 cups grated zucchini

3 cups all-purpose flour

1 tsp. baking soda

¼ tsp. baking powder

1 tsp. salt

3 tsp. cinnamon

  brown sugar

1 Preheat oven to 350 degrees.

2 In a large bowl, mix white sugar, vegetable oil, eggs, and vanilla extract together.

3 Mix in zucchini.

4 Add flour, baking soda, baking powder, salt, and cinnamon and mix until just combined.

5 Divide mixture between 2 greased and floured loaf pans.

6 Sprinkle each loaf with enough brown sugar to lightly coat the top.

7 Bake at 350 degrees for 1 hour or until toothpick inserted in center comes out clean.

Makes 2 loaves.

TO MAKE THE BREAD CHOCOLATE: DECREASE CINNAMON TO 1 TEASPOON, ADD ½ CUP COCOA POWDER, AND OMIT BROWN SUGAR. YOU CAN ADD 1 CUP OF CHOCOLATE CHIPS IF DESIRED. TOSS THE CHIPS WITH A LITTLE FLOUR BEFORE ADDING TO THE MIXTURE. THIS PREVENTS THEM FROM SINKING TO THE BOTTOM OF THE BREAD.

The Best Dinner Rolls

IF I WANT YUMMY ROLLS FOR DINNER, THESE ARE THE ONES I MAKE. THE DOUGH IS DELICIOUS AND TENDER. PLUS, THEY CAN BE MADE IN A LITTLE OVER AN HOUR.

1 pkg. yeast

⅓ cup sugar

1 cup warm water

1 cup warm milk

⅓ cup oil

1 egg

4½ cups flour

½ Tbsp. salt

butter, melted

1 In the bowl of a stand mixer, combine yeast, sugar, and warm water; let mixture sit for 5 minutes until bubbly.

2 Using dough hook, mix in milk, oil, and egg.

3 Add 2 cups flour and mix until combined.

4 Add salt with ½ cup of remaining flour and mix until combined.

5 While mixing continuously, add remaining flour ½ cup at a time until dough begins to pull away from the sides of the bowl.

6 Let dough rise in mixing bowl for about 30 minutes.

7 Form dough into 24 balls and place on greased baking sheet.

8 Let rolls rise for 30 minutes.

9 In preheated oven, bake at 400 degrees for 10–12 minutes until golden brown.

10 Brush hot rolls with melted butter.

Makes 24 rolls.

Mom's Banana Bread

BANANA BREAD IS THE PERFECT WAY TO USE UP THOSE BROWN BANANAS. THIS IS THE RECIPE I GREW UP ON.

½ cup butter, softened

1 cup sugar

2 eggs

3 bananas, mashed

½ cup water

2½ cups flour

1 tsp. baking soda

1 tsp. baking powder

pinch of salt

1 tsp. vanilla

½ cup nuts, chopped (optional)

1 Preheat oven to 375 degrees.

2 In a large bowl, cream together butter and sugar.

3 While mixing, add eggs one at a time until combined.

4 Blend in remaining ingredients and pour into 2 greased medium loaf pans.

5 Bake at 375 degrees for 30–45 minutes until toothpick inserted in center of loaf comes out clean.

Makes 2 loaves.

Banana Nut Muffins

BANANAS AND WALNUTS ARE SUCH A GREAT COMBINATION. THIS PERFECT PAIR HELPS MAKE THIS YUMMY MUFFIN.

⅓ cup sugar

⅓ cup shortening

2 eggs

1¾ cup flour

1 tsp. baking powder

½ tsp. baking soda

½ tsp. salt

1 cup bananas, mashed

½ cup walnuts

1 Preheat oven to 350 degrees.

2 In a medium bowl, cream together sugar and shortening.

3 Add eggs and beat well.

4 In another bowl, whisk together dry ingredients.

5 Add dry ingredients mixture to the cream mixture until just combined.

6 Stir in bananas and walnuts.

7 Spoon batter into greased or lined muffin tins.

8 Bake at 350 degrees for 20 25 minutes.

Makes 12 muffins.

French Bread

THIS IS ONE OF MY GO-TO BREAD RECIPES. IT IS DELICIOUS AND COMES TOGETHER IN ABOUT 1 HOUR.

2¼ cups warm water

2 Tbsp. sugar

2 pkgs. active dry yeast

1 Tbsp. salt

2 Tbsp. canola oil

6 cups flour

1 In the bowl of a stand mixer, combine water and sugar and then sprinkle with yeast. Allow to soften.

2 Add salt, oil, and half of the flour (3 cups); mix well with dough hook. Then mix in remaining flour.

3 Leave dough in the mixer. Allow to rest 10 minutes.

4 Stir dough down and allow to rest for 10 minutes. Repeat this step until dough has been stirred 5 times.

5 Turn dough onto floured surface. Knead 2 or 3 times. Divide dough into 2 balls.

6 Roll each ball of dough into a 9×13-inch rectangle.

7 Roll up from one long end to the other and pinch edges.

8 Place on baking sheet sprayed with cooking spray or sprinkled with cornmeal. Cover and allow to rise 30 minutes.

9 With sharp knife, cut 3 slashes at an angle on top of dough.

10 Bake in preheated oven at 400 degrees for 30 minutes. Check at 20 minutes to avoid overbaking.

Makes 2 loaves.

45-Minute Cinnamon Rolls

WANT HOMEMADE CINNAMON ROLLS BUT DON'T HAVE A LOT OF TIME? THEN THIS IS THE RECIPE FOR YOU.

1 cup + 2 Tbsp. warm water

⅓ cup oil

2 Tbsp. yeast

¼ cup sugar or honey

½ tsp. salt

1 egg

3½ cups flour

Filling:

¼ cup butter, softened

cinnamon

sugar

Icing:

2¼ cups powdered sugar

3 Tbsp. butter, melted

1½ tsp. vanilla extract

1–3 Tbsp. milk

1 In the bowl of a stand mixer, combine water, oil, yeast, and sugar or honey. Allow mixture to rest for 15 minutes.

2 With a dough hook, mix in salt, egg, and 2 cups of the flour until combined.

3 While mixing, add remaining flour ½ cup at a time.

4 Roll dough out into a 9×13-inch rectangle.

5 Spread ¼ cup butter for the filling onto dough.

6 Sprinkle dough generously with cinnamon.

7 Now, sprinkle dough with sugar over the cinnamon. This should also be a generous amount, enough to completely cover the cinnamon so you can't see it.

8 Roll up from one long side to the other to make a log.

9 Cut into 12 slices and arrange on a greased baking sheet.

10 Let rest for 10 minutes.

11 In preheated oven, bake 10–15 minutes at 400 degrees until golden brown.

12 Remove from oven and let the rolls cool slightly.

13 While the rolls are cooling, mix icing ingredients in a small bowl.

14 Spread icing over rolls.

Makes 12 rolls.

Glazed Poppy Seed Bread

POPPY SEED BREAD IS GREAT, BUT THIS GLAZED RECIPE MAKES IT FABULOUS!

3 cups flour

1½ tsp. salt

1½ tsp. baking powder

2½ cups sugar

3 eggs

1½ cups milk

1½ tsp. almond extract

1½ tsp. vanilla extract

1½ tsp. butter flavoring

1 cup + 2 Tbsp. canola oil

¼ cup poppy seeds

Glaze:

¾ cup sugar

¼ cup orange juice

1½ tsp. vanilla

½ tsp. butter flavoring

½ tsp. almond extract

1 Preheat oven to 350 degrees.

2 In a bowl, whisk together flour, salt, baking powder, and sugar until blended well.

3 Add remaining ingredients and mix just until well combined.

4 Pour into ungreased loaf pan and bake at 350 degrees for 45–60 minutes, until a toothpick inserted comes out clean.

5 In a small bowl, mix together glaze ingredients. Pour over bread while still warm.

Makes 1 loaf.

Ice Box Muffins

THIS MUFFIN BATTER WILL KEEP IN THE FRIDGE FOR WEEKS. HOWEVER, THEY ARE SO YUMMY, I DOUBT THEY WILL LAST THAT LONG.

¾ cup sugar

½ cup butter

1 egg

½ tsp. salt

¼ tsp. cinnamon

2 tsp. baking powder

2 cups flour

1 cup milk

Topping:

½ cup brown sugar

1 tsp. cinnamon

¼ cup pecan gems

1 Preheat oven to 350 degrees.

2 In a medium bowl, cream together the sugar and butter.

3 Add egg and blend.

4 In another bowl, whisk together dry ingredients. Alternately add dry mixture and milk to creamed mixture until combined.

5 Cover and refrigerate until ready to bake. The batter will keep in the fridge for 3–4 weeks.

6 Mix together topping ingredients until combined.

7 To bake, spoon batter into greased or lined muffin tins.

8 Fill tins ⅔ full. Sprinkle with topping mixture.

9 Bake at 350 degrees for 18–20 minutes or until golden brown.

Makes 18 muffins.

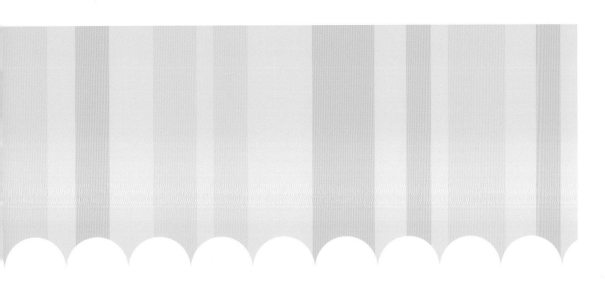

SOUPS AND SALADS

Creamy Chicken Noodle Soup

WHEN IT COMES TO SOUP, THIS IS MY FAMILY'S FAVORITE RECIPE. IT'S NICE AND CREAMY WITH PLENTY OF CHICKEN AND NOODLES.

Base:

2 boneless, skinless chicken breasts

1 tsp. celery salt

1 onion, chopped

2 qts. water

½ tsp. poultry seasoning

2 large carrots, sliced

1 tsp. onion salt

2 celery stalks, sliced

2 tsp. salt

2 cups noodles, uncooked

Cream Sauce:

¾ cup butter

1 cup flour

4 cups milk

   salt and pepper to taste

To make base:

1 In a stockpot, boil base ingredients except noodles for 1 hour.

2 When chicken is tender, remove from broth, cut into 1-inch pieces, and set aside. If the liquid has reduced too much, you can add some more water at this point.

3 Add 2 cups of uncooked noodles and continue to boil for 20 minutes. Make the cream sauce while this cooks.

To make cream sauce:

1 Melt butter in a large saucepan.

2 Whisk in flour, stirring constantly.

3 Gradually add milk, stirring constantly until thickened.

4 Add salt and pepper.

Add cream sauce to base mixture. If the soup is too thin after adding the cream mixture, continue cooking until it reaches desired thickness.

Note: Once your cream sauce has thickened, do not allow it to reach a boil because it may separate. Also, if cream sauce has a strong white sauce flavor, add ½–1 teaspoon lemon juice.

Serves 6–8.

Laura's Potato Salad

THIS IS MY VERSION OF A CLASSIC POTATO SALAD. I TOOK ALL THE THINGS THAT I LOVE IN POTATO SALAD TO CREATE THIS YUMMY COMBINATION.

1 cup mayonnaise

2 Tbsp. sweet relish

¾ tsp. yellow mustard

¾ tsp. salt

1 Tbsp. sugar

2½ lbs. (approx. 5 large) potatoes, baked and peeled. Alternately, you can peel and boil potatoes for approx. 20 minutes.

2 Tbsp. green onion, diced

4 hard-boiled eggs

bacon bits, if desired

1 In a large bowl, mix mayonnaise, sweet relish, yellow mustard, salt, and sugar together.

2 Add potatoes, green onion, and eggs. Combine and refrigerate at least 1 hour.

3 Mix in bacon just before serving.

Serves 10.

Luau Fruit Salad

THIS SALAD HAS A NICE TROPICAL FLAIR. YOU CAN ALSO LEAVE OUT ALL THE FRUIT
AND USE THE BASE AS A FRUIT DIP FOR FRESH FRUIT.

1 (3.4-oz.) pkg. coconut cream
   pudding mix

1 cup buttermilk

1 (8-oz.) container whipped
   topping

1 banana, sliced

1 apple, diced

1 (15-oz.) can pineapple
   tidbits, drained

1 (11-oz.) can mandarin
   oranges, drained

½ cup toasted coconut, if
   desired

1 In a large bowl, whisk dry pudding mix and
   buttermilk together for 2 minutes.

2 Fold in whipped topping.

3 Mix in fruit.

4 Top with toasted coconut just before serving.

Serves 6–8.

LAURA POWELL • 57

Clam Chowder

THIS SOUP COMES FROM MY MOM. IT WAS A FAVORITE FOR MY BROTHERS AND ME WHILE GROWING UP. IT'S A VERY RICH AND CREAMY CHOWDER. THIS IS NOW A FAVORITE FOR MY FAMILY, AND MOST OF MY FAMILY ARE NOT SEAFOOD FANS.

1 cup minced onion

1 cup chopped celery

2–3 cups diced potatoes

2 cans minced clams (undrained)

¾ cup butter

¾ cup flour

1 qt. half-and-half

1½ tsp. salt

pinch of pepper

½ tsp. sugar

1 In a stockpot, add onion, celery, and potatoes. Add enough water to cover ingredients and cook on medium for 20 minutes or until tender. During last 5 minutes of cooking, add clam juice from canned clams.

2 In a separate saucepan, melt butter and add flour. Cook for 2 minutes, stirring constantly.

3 Add half-and-half, salt, pepper, and sugar. Cook until thick.

4 Add cream sauce to cooked vegetables and cook until thick.

5 Add clams and stir for 2 minutes.

Serves 6–8.

Sweet Chili

WHEN I WAS GROWING UP, EVERY YEAR FOR HALLOWEEN MY MOM WOULD MAKE HOMEMADE CHILI. SINCE HAVING MY OWN CHILDREN, I DECIDED TO CARRY ON THE TRADITION. THIS IS THE QUICKER VERSION THAT I CREATED FROM MY MOM'S ORIGINAL.

1 lb. hamburger

1 medium onion

5 (15-oz.) cans kidney beans, undrained

2 (6-oz.) cans tomato paste

2 (10¾-oz.) cans condensed tomato soup

4 tsp. chili powder

¾ cup brown sugar

1 In a stockpot, brown hamburger and onion until beef is no longer pink; drain.

2 Add remaining ingredients and simmer for 1 hour.

Serves 6–8.

Cucumber Salad

THIS IS A GREAT SALAD TO MAKE IF YOU HAVE A SUMMER VEGETABLE GARDEN. YOU CAN USE UP THOSE TOMATOES AND CUCUMBERS, AND IT'S PERFECT TO TAKE TO A BARBECUE.

5   large cucumbers, sliced

2   tomatoes, diced

½   cup onion, minced

¾   cup vinegar

⅓   cup oil

I   Tbsp. lemon juice

I   tsp. salt (or more, if desired)

I   tsp. pepper

I   Tbsp. sugar

I   Tbsp. parsley, chopped

I In a 9×13 baking dish, layer half the cucumbers followed by half the tomatoes and onion.

2 Repeat step I with the other half of the cucumbers, tomatoes, and onion.

3 Mix together the remaining ingredients in a small bowl and pour over layers.

4 Let salad soak 6–8 hours in the refrigerator, stirring halfway through.

Serves 10–12.

Bow Tie Chicken Salad

THIS IS AN ALL-TIME FAVORITE PASTA SALAD OF MINE. I LOVE IT. IT IS ESPECIALLY GOOD TO USE FOR BRIDAL AND BABY SHOWERS.

1½ cups bow tie pasta, uncooked

1½ cups rotini pasta, uncooked

1½ cups diced cooked chicken

1 (20-oz.) can pineapple, drained

1 cup red grapes, sliced in half

2 ribs of celery, diced

3 green onions, diced

1 cup dried cranberries

½ cup sugar

1 cup mayonnaise

1 cup cashews (if desired)

1 Cook pasta according to package directions. Drain and cool pasta.

2 In a large bowl, toss pasta, chicken, pineapple, grapes, celery, onions, and dried cranberries.

3 In a separate bowl, mix sugar and mayonnaise.

4 Pour mayonnaise mixture over pasta mixture and toss.

5 Refrigerate for 2 hours before serving. Mix in cashews just before serving.

Serves 8–10.

Marinated Zucchini

THIS IS A QUICK AND EASY WAY TO ENJOY THAT FRESH SUMMER ZUCCHINI. YOU CAN ALSO USE YELLOW SUMMER SQUASH.

2 small zucchini sliced into thin coins about ¼ inch thick.

⅔ cup sun dried tomato vinaigrette with roasted red peppers

1 Put zucchini in a 9×9 dish.

2 Cover the zucchini with dressing and toss to coat.

3 Cover dish and place in the refrigerator for at least 24 hours. You can give it a stir or two during the 24 hours, but it's not necessary.

Serves 6.

Pineapple Coleslaw

THIS IS A QUICK AND EASY COLESLAW THAT GETS ITS SWEETNESS FROM CRUSHED PINEAPPLE. IT'S PERFECT FOR THOSE SUMMER MEALS.

3 cups coleslaw salad mix

1 cup drained, unsweetened crushed pineapple

⅓ cup mayonnaise

¼ tsp. celery seed

1 In a bowl, toss together coleslaw mix and pineapple.

2 In a small bowl, mix mayonnaise and celery seed together.

3 Pour over coleslaw and toss to coat.

4 Cover and refrigerate for at least 1 hour.

Serves 6.

Easy Cheesy Veggie Soup

THIS SOUP RECIPE IS ONE I CREATED ON A NIGHT I NEEDED A QUICK DINNER. IT CAN'T GET ANY EASIER THAN 6 INGREDIENTS. THIS SOUP WAS QUICK, EASY, AND OH SO CHEESY.

3½ cups water

2 (10¾-oz.) cans cream of chicken soup

½ onion, diced

2 potatoes, peeled and diced

1 (16-oz.) pkg. California blend frozen vegetables, thawed

1 (16-oz.) pkg. Velveeta®, cubed

1 In a soup pot, mix water and canned soup until smooth.

2 Stir in onion and potato.

3 Bring to a boil and then reduce heat and simmer for 10 minutes, stirring occasionally.

4 Add thawed vegetables and bring back to a boil.

5 Reduce heat and simmer for another 8–10 minutes until potatoes are tender, stirring occasionally.

6 Remove from heat and stir in cubed Velveeta® until melted.

Serves 6.

Frozen Fruit Salad

THIS FROZEN SALAD IS COLD AND REFRESHING. IT'S GREAT TO SERVE AS A SUMMER DESSERT.

1 (20-oz.) can crushed pineapple

2 bananas

1 (8-oz.) pkg. cream cheese, softened

¾ cup sugar

1 (12-oz.) container whipped topping

1 (16-oz.) pkg. frozen strawberries

1 Drain can of pineapple well, reserving juice.

2 Slice bananas and let soak in reserved pineapple juice.

3 With a hand mixer, beat cream cheese and sugar together in a large bowl.

4 Once combined, beat in whipped topping.

5 Drain bananas and fold all of the fruits into the creamy mixture.

6 Pour into a 9×13 pan and spread evenly. Cover tightly with foil and freeze.

7 Allow salad to thaw slightly before serving and cut into squares.

Serves 12.

Oriental Chicken Salad

THIS IS MY FAVORITE ORIENTAL CHICKEN SALAD. I LOVE ALL THE CRUNCHY ADDITIONS TO IT.

Dressing:

- 2 Tbsp. sugar
- 1 tsp. salt
- ½ tsp. pepper
- 3 Tbsp. rice vinegar
- ¼ cup oil

Salad:

- 2 cups soy sauce
- 2 Tbsp. sugar
- 4 boneless skinless chicken breasts
- 2 oz. wonton wraps
- ¼ of a 6.75-oz. pkg. rice stick
- 1½ heads of lettuce, chopped
- 4 green onions, diced at an angle
- 2 Tbsp. toasted sesame seeds

1 Preheat oven to 350 degrees.

2 In a bowl, combine dressing ingredients except oil.

3 Slowly whisk in oil until well combined.

4 Store in the refrigerator until serving time.

5 In a small bowl, combine soy sauce and sugar.

6 Place chicken in a 9×13 baking dish and pour soy sauce mixture over chicken. Bake at 350 degrees for 1 hour until juices run clear.

7 Meanwhile, cut wonton wraps into small strips using a knife or pizza cutter.

8 Deep fry strips in hot oil until crisp and brown.

9 Deep fry rice stick until puffed.

10 When chicken is fully cooked, remove it from pan and allow to cool.

11 Once chicken has cooled, dice into bite-sized pieces.

12 Place lettuce, green onion, and chicken in a large bowl and toss with enough dressing to coat.

13 Place rice stick, wonton strips, and sesame seeds on top of salad and serve.

Serves 10–15.

Rice-A-Roni Chicken Salad

THIS SALAD IS A PERFECT DISH FOR A SUMMER MEAL. IT'S ALSO WONDERFUL TO SERVE AT A LUNCHEON. I LOVE THE FLAVOR OF THIS SALAD, AND MOST OF THE FLAVOR COMES FROM A BOX OF RICE-A-RONI®.

2 (6.9-oz.) boxes of Rice-A-Roni® fried rice, cooked according to package and cooled

1 lb. mushrooms, sliced

1–2 Tbsp. butter

4 chicken breasts, cooked and diced

1 cup celery, diced

1 cup green onion, diced

1 cup mayonnaise

1 While you are cooking the Rice-A-Roni®, sauté mushroom slices in butter until tender.

2 Allow mushrooms to cool along with the cooked Rice-A-Roni®.

3 In a large bowl, combine cooled Rice-A-Roni®, sautéed mushrooms, and remaining ingredients. Stir until well combined. Refrigerate for at least 30 minutes before serving.

Serves 6–8.

Mama Mia's Minestrone Soup

THIS MINESTRONE SOUP IS A LITTLE DIFFERENT BECAUSE IT ALL STARTS WITH SOME BACON, WHICH GIVES THIS SOUP WONDERFUL FLAVOR.

½ lb. bacon

1 large onion, chopped

1 cup celery, chopped

2 (14.5-oz.) cans Italian stewed tomatoes

2 (14.5-oz.) cans beef broth

2 (5.5-oz.) cans tomato juice

1 (15-oz.) can northern white beans, drained and rinsed

1 (14.5-oz.) can green beans, undrained

3 carrots, cut into chunks

2 cups cabbage, shredded (do not use the precut coleslaw mix)

2 cups water

½ tsp. thyme

¼ tsp. basil

¼ tsp. oregano

1 cup macaroni, uncooked

Parmesan cheese, shredded

1 Cook bacon in a skillet until crisp and set aside.

2 Sauté the onion and celery in bacon grease until tender.

3 In a stockpot, combine celery and onion mixture.

4 Add stewed tomatoes, beef broth, tomato juice, white beans, green beans, carrots, cabbage, water, thyme, basil, and oregano.

5 Crumble bacon and add to the pot.

6 Bring to a boil and then reduce to a simmer.

7 Simmer until vegetables are tender. Then add macaroni and cook until tender.

8 Top each bowl with Parmesan cheese and serve.

Serves 10–12.

Chili Cheese Fritos® Salad

I HAD THIS AT A POTLUCK DINNER WITH THE LADIES IN MY CHURCH. THE GIRL WHO BROUGHT IT TOLD ME HOW EASY IT WAS AND WHAT WAS IN IT, SO I CREATED MY OWN VERSION THE NEXT DAY.

3   (14-oz.) cans corn, drained

¼   red pepper, diced

¼   green pepper, diced

¼   red onion, diced

1   cup cheddar cheese, grated

1¼ cup mayonnaise

1   (9¼-oz.) bag Chili Cheese Fritos®

1 Combine corn, peppers, onion, cheese, and mayonnaise in a bowl.

2 Place in the refrigerator until ready to serve.

3 Just before serving, mix in Fritos®, saving about a handful to sprinkle on top.

Serves 8–10.

Shrimp Salad

THIS RECIPE IS A FAMILY FAVORITE. YOU CAN FIND IT AT MANY OF OUR FAMILY GATHERINGS. THE RECIPE ORIGINATED FROM MY GRANDMOTHER'S NEIGHBOR, MARILYN. THEN MY MOTHER ADAPTED IT SLIGHTLY BY ADDING THE DILL WEED AND CELERY TO THE RECIPE. I DEFINITELY THINK THAT THE DILL WEED MAKES THIS SALAD FABULOUS.

2½ cups salad macaroni, uncooked

3 qts. boiling water

1 tsp. butter

1 tsp. vinegar

½ tsp. garlic salt

½ tsp. onion salt

dash of celery salt

1–3 green onions, chopped

3 hard-boiled eggs, chopped

2 cans of shrimp or 6–8 oz. small, frozen, fully cooked shrimp, thawed according to package directions

1 rib celery, diced fine

1 cup of mayonnaise

1 tsp. dill weed + extra for garnish

2 Tbsp.–¼ cup milk

1 Cook salad macaroni in boiling water along with butter according to package directions until tender.

2 Drain and add to a large bowl.

3 Mix in the vinegar, garlic salt, onion salt, and celery salt.

4 Refrigerate mixture for several hours or overnight.

5 Before serving, mix in the green onion, hard-boiled eggs, shrimp, celery, mayonnaise, dill weed, and enough milk to make smooth and creamy.

6 Sprinkle with additional dill weed for garnish.

Serves 10–12.

Creamy Piña Colada Salad

I LOVE PIÑA COLADAS AND THOUGHT THEY WOULD MAKE A GREAT SALAD. IT TURNED OUT DELICIOUS AND WAS LIKED BY ALL. IT IS VERY SIMPLE TO WHIP TOGETHER. YOU JUST NEED AN HOUR TO LET IT SIT IN THE FRIDGE BEFORE SERVING.

1 (12-oz.) container whipped topping

1 (3.4-oz.) pkg. instant coconut cream or vanilla pudding mix

3 (6-oz.) piña colada yogurts

2–3 bananas, sliced

1 (20-oz.) can pineapple tidbits, drained

toasted coconut (optional)

1 In a large bowl, mix whipped topping, dry pudding mix, and yogurt.

2 Mix well to dissolve pudding mix.

3 Refrigerate mixture for at least 1 hour. (This helps the pudding fully dissolve.)

4 Mix in bananas and pineapple just before serving.

5 Sprinkle top with toasted coconut, if desired.

Serves 8.

Luncheon Salad with Pretty in Pink Dressing

THIS IS A RECIPE THAT CAME FROM MY AUNT. YOU CAN SERVE IT WITH THE CHICKEN AS A MAIN DISH. IT'S ALSO GREAT AS A SIDE SALAD.

1 (10-oz.) bag romaine lettuce

1 (10-oz.) bag Mediterranean salad mix

1 (10-oz.) bag spinach

1½ cups fresh Parmesan cheese

2 cups shredded mozzarella cheese

½–1 lb. bacon, cooked and crumbled

½ cup roasted slivered almonds

6 cooked chicken breasts that have been marinated in teriyaki sauce, diced (optional)

Additional mix-ins:

dried cranberries

diced red apple

extra almonds

Pretty in Pink Dressing:

1 cup sugar

½ cup red wine vinegar

1 tsp. dry mustard

1½ tsp. salt

½ cup red onion, chopped

1 cup canola oil

Salad:

Toss salad ingredients together and serve salad with Pretty in Pink dressing.

Pretty in Pink Dressing:

Add Pretty in Pink dressing ingredients (except canola oil) to a blender. Turn on blender and through opening in blender lid, slowly add 1 cup canola oil while blending. Blend until onion is all chopped into dressing and is well blended with the oil.

Serves 15–18.

Simple Chicken Salad Croissant Sandwiches

DURING THE SUMMER, I LOVE TO MAKE SANDWICHES AND SALADS FOR MY DINNER MENU. THERE'S NO NEED TO HEAT UP THE KITCHEN, AND ON A HOT DAY, IT'S NICE TO EAT SOMETHING COOL AND FRESH. I ALSO SERVE IT FOR SHOWERS, GET-TOGETHERS, AND SO ON. THIS MAKES ENOUGH FOR MY FAMILY FOR DINNER, AND WE HAVE LEFTOVERS FOR LUNCH THE NEXT DAY.

3   cups cooked chicken, diced

1   cup celery, diced

1   green onion, diced

4   hard-boiled eggs, diced

1   cup mayonnaise

¼   cup Miracle Whip®

1   Tbsp. lemon juice

¼   tsp. salt

10–12 large croissants

    lettuce leaves

¾   cup cashews

1 In a large bowl, mix chicken, celery, onion, eggs, mayonnaise, Miracle Whip®, lemon juice, and salt together.

2 Slice open croissants and on one half of each croissant, place a piece of lettuce followed by the chicken mixture.

3 Sprinkle with cashews and top with other half of croissant.

Serves 10–12.

MAIN DISHES

Creamy Italian Chicken

THIS IS A RECIPE THAT MY BEST FRIEND FROM HIGH SCHOOL PASSED ALONG TO ME YEARS AGO. IT IS SO SIMPLE AND EASY, PLUS IT'S DONE IN YOUR SLOW COOKER! YOU CAN LEAVE THE CHICKEN BREASTS WHOLE WHEN YOU SERVE THEM, BUT I PREFER TO SHRED THE CHICKEN AND PUT IT BACK IN THE SAUCE.

4–6 chicken breasts

1 packet dry Italian dressing mix

1 (8-oz.) pkg. cream cheese, softened

2 (10¾-oz.) cans condensed cream of chicken soup

1 Put chicken breasts in a Crock-Pot®. Sprinkle with dry Italian dressing mix.

2 Mix cream cheese and soup in a separate bowl. Pour over chicken.

3 Cook on low all day (8 hours). Shred or serve whole breasts over rice or noodles. (Add milk if needed to thin sauce out.)

Serves 4–6.

Hubby's Favorite Casserole

THIS IS MY HUSBAND'S FAVORITE CASSEROLE THAT HIS MOTHER WOULD MAKE HIM WHILE GROWING UP, HENCE THE NAME "HUBBY'S FAVORITE CASSEROLE." THE RECIPE IS SIMPLE AND BASIC, AND MY WHOLE FAMILY LIKES IT.

1 lb. hamburger

½ onion, diced

1 (10¾-oz.) can condensed tomato soup

1½ cups water

2 cups egg noodles, uncooked

1 (14.5-oz.) can corn, drained

salt and pepper to taste

1 cup cheddar cheese, shredded

1 Preheat oven to 350 degrees.

2 In a large skillet, brown hamburger with onion; drain.

3 Mix in tomato soup and water and bring to a boil.

4 Add noodles and cook for 10 minutes covered, stirring occasionally.

5 Mix in corn and salt and pepper to taste.

6 Put half of mixture in a 2-quart casserole dish and cover with ½ cup of cheese.

7 Put remaining noodle mixture in a casserole dish and top with remaining cheese.

8 Cook at 350 degrees, covered, for 25 minutes.

9 Uncover and cook another 5 minutes.

Serves 4–6.

Open-Faced Sloppy Joes

THIS IS A TWIST ON YOUR REGULAR SLOPPY JOE RECIPE. IT'S A QUICK AND EASY DINNER AND ONLY TAKES 6 INGREDIENTS.

1 (16.3-oz.) can refrigerated large buttermilk biscuits

1 lb. hamburger

½ cup green onion, sliced

1 (15½-oz.) can sloppy joe sandwich sauce

1 (11-oz.) can whole kernel corn with red and green peppers, undrained

fresh cilantro, chopped (optional)

1 Bake biscuits according to package directions.

2 While biscuits bake, brown hamburger in a skillet; drain.

3 Add green onion, sloppy joe sauce, and corn to beef in skillet. Mix well to combine.

4 Cook for 2–3 minutes or until heated through.

5 To serve, split biscuits in half and place a spoonful of the beef mixture over each half. Sprinkle with fresh cilantro, if desired.

Serves 8.

Reuben Sandwich

THIS IS A YUMMY SANDWICH THAT'S PERFECT FOR ST. PATRICK'S DAY. YOU CAN MAKE IT USING FROZEN BREAD DOUGH OR WITH MY HOMEMADE DOUGH RECIPE ON THE NEXT PAGE. IT IS SO SIMPLE TO MAKE. YOU CAN ALSO USE THIS RECIPE AND CHANGE UP THE SANDWICH INGREDIENTS FOR WHATEVER YOU HAVE ON HAND.

1 loaf frozen bread dough, thawed; or make the homemade dough recipe on the next page

¼ cup Thousand Island dressing + extra for dipping

8 slices Swiss cheese

½ lb. corned beef or pastrami

caraway seeds (optional)

1 Preheat oven to 350 degrees (or temperature listed on the package of your frozen bread dough).

2 Roll your bread dough out to a 9×13-inch rectangle.

3 Transfer to a baking pan sprayed with cooking spray.

4 Using kitchen shears or a pizza cutter, from the long side make 3-inch-long cuts 1 inch apart toward the center. Repeat with the other long side.

5 Down the center section of the dough, spread the Thousand Island dressing and top with cheese and meat.

6 Start with one end of the dough and pull one strip on each side together, twist together in the center, and tuck ends under. It will make a little knot shape. Repeat the process with all the remaining strips.

7 Roll the ends of the dough up to seal the end of the loaf. You don't want any of the sandwich filling coming out during the baking process.

8 If you want to get that rye bread flavor, you can sprinkle on some caraway seeds at this point.

9 Bake for 30–35 minutes until nice and golden.

10 Allow to cool a few minutes before slicing. Cut into slices and serve with extra Thousand Island dressing, if desired.

Serves 6–8.

Bread Dough:

1 cup + 2 Tbsp. warm water

⅓ cup oil

2 Tbsp. yeast

¼ cup sugar or honey

½ tsp. salt

1 egg

3½ cups flour

1 Combine water, oil, yeast, and sugar or honey together. Let rest for 15 minutes.

2 Mix in the salt and egg.

3 Gradually add flour.

4 Your dough is ready to use for the Reuben sandwich now. Just make sure you use a good amount of flour when rolling out the dough. This dough is quite sticky.

Biscuit Waffle Breakfast Sandwich

THIS IS A FUN TWIST ON A MORNING BISCUIT SANDWICH. INSTEAD OF BAKING YOUR BISCUIT, YOU COOK THEM IN A WAFFLE IRON. AND INSTEAD OF SCRAMBLING EGGS ON THE STOVE TOP, YOU BAKE THEM IN THE OVEN.

2   Tbsp. butter or margarine

¼   cup sweet onion, chopped

¼   cup red or green pepper, diced

6   large eggs

¼   cup whipping cream

½   tsp. salt

¼   tsp. pepper

1   cup (4 oz.) sharp cheddar cheese, shredded

1   can (16.3-oz.) refrigerated large buttermilk biscuits

4   cooked sausage patties or whatever meat you prefer

1 Preheat oven to 425 degrees.

2 Place butter, onion, and red or green pepper in a lightly greased 9×9 pan. Bake for 7–8 minutes.

3 Meanwhile, whisk together eggs, cream, salt, and pepper in a medium bowl.

4 When onion and peppers are cooked and softened, pour egg mixture into the square pan and sprinkle with cheese.

5 At this point, you could sprinkle in about ½ cup cooked bacon, sausage, or ham instead of using the sausage patties. Bake at 425 degrees for 12 minutes or until set.

6 Open biscuits and flatten each biscuit by rolling out to a 4-inch piece.

7 Preheat a square Belgian waffle maker or regular waffle maker.

8 One at a time, place biscuits on hot waffle maker and close. Cook for about 2 minutes or until golden brown. Set aside when cooked.

9 When egg mixture is done cooking, let stand 10 minutes.

10 Cut into 4 squares. Serve egg sandwiched between 2 biscuit waffles along with cooked sausage patties.

Serves 4.

Too Easy Chicken Tacos

THIS IS THE EASIEST WAY TO MAKE CHICKEN TACOS. IT IS ONE OF MY CHILDREN'S FAVORITE WAYS TO EAT TACOS.

1 lb. chicken breasts or tenders, frozen	1 Place chicken in a Crock-Pot® with water and sprinkle with the seasoning mix.
¼ cup water	2 Cook on low for 6–8 hours.
1 pkg. McCormick® chicken taco seasoning mix	3 Shred chicken and put back in the Crock-Pot® to mix with remaining juices.
	4 Serve on tacos with your favorite toppings.
	Serves 6.

Mom's Sloppy Joes

THIS IS A RECIPE MY MOM HAS MADE AS LONG AS I CAN REMEMBER, AND I HAVE BEEN MAKING IT SINCE I GOT MARRIED. IT'S VERY QUICK AND SIMPLE. I LIKE TO USE BARBECUE SAUCE WITH A SMOKY OR HICKORY FLAVOR TO IT.

1 lb. hamburger

¼–½ cup onion, chopped

1 (10¾-oz.) can condensed tomato soup

3 Tbsp. sugar

2 Tbsp. barbecue sauce (or more, if desired)

8 hamburger buns

8 slices of American cheese (optional)

1 In a skillet, brown the hamburger with the onion.

2 Add the soup, sugar, and barbecue sauce and simmer for 5 minutes. You can add more barbecue sauce to make it the consistency you like.

3 Serve on buns with a slice of American cheese, if desired.

Serves 8.

Laura's Sweet Pork

THERE IS A MEXICAN RESTAURANT WHERE I LIVE THAT SERVES DELICIOUS SWEET PORK THAT MY FAMILY IS ADDICTED TO. I CREATED THIS AT-HOME VERSION TO HELP US CUT DOWN THE COST OF THAT ADDICTION AND MAKE OUR OWN. MAKE EXTRA TO USE IN MY SWEET PORK QUESADILLAS ON PAGE 102.

2–4 lb. pork roast

1 can cola (not diet)

1 (10-oz.) can enchilada sauce

2 cloves garlic, minced

1 (4-oz.) can diced green chilies

1 cup brown sugar

1 In a gallon-sized resealable bag, marinate roast in cola overnight.

2 Place roast along with leftover marinade in a Crock-Pot® and cook on low until very tender (about 8 hours).

3 Drain off any liquid after cooking.

4 Shred pork and place back in the Crock-Pot®.

5 Mix in enchilada sauce, garlic, green chilies, and brown sugar.

6 Continue to cook on low for 30 more minutes to 1 hour.

7 Serve meat in soft flour shells with taco toppings.

Serves 8–16.

Poppy Seed Chicken

THIS RECIPE IS ONE THAT I GOT FROM A NEIGHBOR BEFORE MY WEDDING. I HAVE BEEN MAKING THIS NOW FOR OVER 16 YEARS. IT'S A FAMILY FAVORITE AND IS ONE OF THOSE SIMPLE RECIPES FOR THOSE BUSY NIGHTS. IT CALLS FOR 6 INGREDIENTS, PLUS THE COOKED RICE THAT YOU SERVE IT OVER. IT'S ALSO AN EXCELLENT WAY TO USE UP LEFTOVER CHICKEN. THIS IS GOOD, CREAMY, COMFORT FOOD!

1 (10¾-oz.) can cream of chicken soup

1½ cups sour cream

3 cups cooked chicken, diced

1 cellophane sleeve of Ritz® crackers, crushed

1 Tbsp. poppy seeds

4 Tbsp. butter, melted

1 Preheat oven to 350 degrees.

2 In a bowl, mix together soup and sour cream until well blended.

3 Stir in diced chicken.

4 Spread creamy chicken mixture into a 9×9 baking dish.

5 In a large resealable bag, crush crackers. Then add poppy seeds and butter to bag and seal. Toss to coat.

6 Sprinkle cracker mixture over chicken.

7 Bake at 350 degrees for 30 minutes.

8 Serve over cooked rice.

Serves 4–6.

Quick Sweet and Sour Meatballs

THIS IS A QUICK DINNER. IT CAN ALSO BE TURNED INTO AN APPETIZER BY JUST REDUCING THE KETCHUP AND GRAPE JELLY TO ½ CUP EACH.

¾ cup ketchup

¾ cup grape jelly

1 (16-oz.) pkg. precooked frozen meatballs, thawed

1 In a skillet, combine ketchup and grape jelly.

2 Heat over medium heat, stirring frequently until grape jelly is dissolved.

3 Add meatballs and stir to coat.

4 Continue stirring until meatballs are heated through.

5 Serve over cooked rice.

Serves 4–6.

Saucy Boneless Ribs

THESE SAUCY RIBS ARE MADE IN THE OVEN. THEY ARE GREAT SERVED WITH A POTATO DISH ON THE SIDE OR THEY CAN ALSO BE SERVED OVER RICE.

4 lbs. boneless pork ribs

2 cups ketchup

1 cup brown sugar

1 cup onion, chopped

2 Tbsp. prepared mustard

2 Tbsp. Worcestershire sauce

1 Preheat oven to 350 degrees.

2 Brown ribs in a skillet and place in a baking dish.

3 In a small bowl, mix remaining ingredients together for the sauce and pour over meat.

4 Bake at 350 degrees, covered, for 2 hours.

5 Uncover and bake 1 more hour.

Serves 6–8.

Hawaiian Haystacks

THIS RECIPE IS A STAPLE IN MY HOUSE. IT'S A FAVORITE OF ALL MY CHILDREN. IT IS ALSO FUN TO SERVE AT FAMILY GET-TOGETHERS. MOST OF THE TIME WHEN I USE THE STOVE-TOP METHOD, I DON'T EVEN ADD CHICKEN TO THE SAUCE.

Stove-top method for sauce:

2 (10¾-oz.) cans condensed cream of chicken soup

1 can milk

2 cups cooked chicken breasts, diced or shredded

1 Heat soup and milk on the stove until heated thoroughly. You want this to be the consistency of gravy. You can add more milk if the mixture is too thick.

2 Add cooked chicken and continue to heat until chicken is warm.

Crock-Pot® method for sauce:

2 frozen chicken breasts

2 (10¾-oz.) cans condensed cream of chicken soup

milk

1 Place chicken breasts in the Crock-Pot® and cover with soup.

2 Cook on low for 6–8 hours.

3 Remove chicken from the Crock-Pot® and shred or dice the chicken. Return to the Crock-Pot®.

4 Add enough milk to the soup and chicken to make the consistency of gravy.

Serve the sauce over cooked rice. Then top with any of the following toppings. Serves 6–8.

shredded cheddar cheese	sliced almonds	raisins
pineapple tidbits	diced fresh mushroom	diced green pepper
sliced olives	chow mein noodles	water chestnuts
diced green onion	diced tomatoes	cashews
chopped celery	peas	soy sauce
shredded coconut	mandarin oranges	anything else that you like

Sweet Pork Quesadillas

I LOVE MAKING QUESADILLAS WITH LEFTOVER MEAT. THIS VERSION IS THE PERFECT WAY
TO USE ANY LEFTOVER LAURA'S SWEET PORK YOU MAY HAVE.

6 (10-inch) tortillas

2 Tbsp. butter, melted

cheddar cheese, shredded

green onion, diced

leftover Laura's Sweet Pork,
warmed (see page 95)

1 Brush one side of each tortilla with melted
butter.

2 Place tortilla butter side down in a frying pan.

3 Sprinkle entire tortilla with a light layer of
cheddar cheese and sprinkle on some green onion.

4 Cook over medium heat until underside is
browned and crisp and cheese is melted.

5 Top half the tortilla with warmed sweet pork
and fold tortilla in half. Then cut in half so you have
two triangles.

6 Repeat steps 1–5 with remaining tortillas.

Serves 6.

Baked Oven Omelet

THIS RECIPE COMES FROM MY MOM. SHE HAS MADE THIS AS LONG AS I CAN REMEMBER. THE GREAT THING ABOUT THIS IS YOU CAN MAKE IT THE NIGHT BEFORE AND HAVE IT ALL READY IN THE MORNING. I LIKE TO BUY THE SANDWICH BREAD THAT IS IN THE SHAPE OF A SQUARE TO MAKE THIS. IT MAKES IT EASIER.

1 loaf sandwich bread

butter

3 cups sharp cheddar cheese, grated

2 cups chopped ham

¼ cup green onion, chopped

5 eggs, beaten

2⅓ cups milk

1 tsp. salt

1 tsp. paprika

1 Tbsp. prepared mustard

1 Trim crust off bread.

2 Butter both sides of each slice of bread.

3 Place just enough buttered slices to cover the bottom of a 9×13 pan.

4 Top bread layer with 1 cup cheese, half the ham, and half the green onion.

5 Place another layer of buttered bread slices.

6 Layer again with 1 cup cheese, remaining ham, and remaining green onion.

7 In a medium bowl, beat egg, milk, salt, paprika, and mustard together.

8 Pour over layers in the pan.

9 Top with remaining cheese and refrigerate overnight.

10 Bake in preheated oven at 350 degrees, uncovered, for 45–60 minutes until knife comes out clean.

Serves 9–12.

Roast Beef Casserole

THIS RECIPE IS AN EXCELLENT WAY TO USE UP LEFTOVER ROAST BEEF AND WAS GIVEN TO ME BY MY MOTHER-IN-LAW.

1–2 cups leftover roast beef, cut up

¼ lb. cheese, cubed

1 (10¾-oz.) can cream of chicken soup

2 cups dry noodles, cooked per package directions

green pepper, diced (optional)

1 Preheat oven to 350 degrees.

2 Combine ingredients and place in an 8×8 casserole dish.

3 Bake at 350 degrees, uncovered, for 30–45 minutes until hot and bubbly.

Serves 4.

Chicken Tetrazzini

THIS IS ONE OF MY ALL-TIME FAVORITE COMFORT DISHES. IT IS RICH AND CREAMY. I LOVE THE FRESH MUSHROOMS IN IT.

8   oz. fresh mushrooms, sliced

6   green onions, chopped

2   Tbsp. butter

¾   cup butter

2½ cups whipping cream or half-and-half

3   Tbsp. flour

1½ cups sour cream

    salt and pepper, to taste

1   (12-oz.) pkg. medium egg noodles, cooked according to package instructions

4   chicken breasts, cooked and cubed

3   oz. Parmesan cheese

1 Preheat oven to 300 degrees.

2 In a skillet, sauté mushrooms and green onion in 2 tablespoons butter and set aside.

3 Combine remaining butter, whipping cream, and flour in a saucepan and cook over medium heat until it starts to thicken.

4 Remove from heat and mix in sour cream plus salt and pepper to taste.

5 Mix sauce with cooked noodles, cooked chicken, sautéed mushrooms, and green onion.

6 Pour half the noodle mixture into a 9×13 pan and layer on half of the Parmesan cheese.

7 Cover with remaining noodle mixture and top with remaining Parmesan cheese.

8 Bake at 300 degrees, uncovered, for 45 minutes.

Serves 8.

Red and White Baked Pasta

THIS IS A DISH THAT IS PERFECT FOR THOSE REALLY BUSY NIGHTS. WITH ONLY 5 INGREDIENTS, IT COMES TOGETHER QUICKLY AND IS A FAMILY PLEASER.

4   cups penne pasta

1   (15-oz.) jar Alfredo sauce

1   (24-oz.) jar marinara sauce

2   cups mozzarella cheese, shredded

1   cup Parmesan cheese, shredded

1 Preheat oven to 350 degrees.

2 Cook and drain pasta according to package directions.

3 In a large bowl, combine the two sauces and cheese. Stir until well combined.

4 Mix in the cooked pasta and place mixture into a 9×13 baking dish.

5 Bake uncovered for 20–25 minutes until bubbly.

6 Sprinkle with Parmesan cheese and bake for another 5 minutes.

Serves 6–8.

Sour Cream Chicken Enchiladas

MY GRANDMOTHER USED TO MAKE YUMMY CHICKEN ENCHILADAS, AND WE WOULD
REQUEST HER DISH OFTEN. THIS IS A SIMPLIFIED VERSION OF HER ORIGINAL RECIPE.

2 (10¾-oz. each) cans condensed cream of chicken soup

1 (4-oz.) can diced green chilies

3–4 green onions, sliced

2 cups sour cream

1 small can sliced olives, drained

4 large chicken breasts, cooked and shredded or diced

1–2 cups Monterey Jack cheese, shredded

12 (10-inch) flour tortillas

2 cups cheddar cheese, shredded

1 Preheat oven to 350 degrees.

2 In a bowl, combine soup, chilies, onions, sour cream, and olives.

3 Place 2 cups of soup mixture into another bowl and set aside.

4 Add chicken and Monterey Jack cheese to remaining mixture.

5 Fill tortillas with cheesy chicken mixture, then roll up and place in a 9×13 baking dish.

6 Spread the remaining 2 cups of soup mixture over the top of the rolled enchiladas and sprinkle with cheddar cheese.

7 Bake uncovered for 20–30 minutes until hot and bubbly.

Serves 12.

Chicken Pillows

THIS RECIPE IS ANOTHER FAMILY FAVORITE AND WAS A FAVORITE OF MINE AS A CHILD.
IT'S A GREAT USE FOR LEFTOVER CHICKEN.

Pillows:

6 oz. cream cheese, softened

¼ cup green onion, diced

⅓ cup mushrooms, chopped

2 Tbsp. butter, softened

¼ tsp. salt

dash of pepper

3–4 cups chicken, cooked and cubed

2 cans crescent rolls

½ cup butter, melted

bread crumbs

Cream sauce:

1 (10¾-oz.) can cream of chicken soup

1 cup sour cream

⅛ tsp. curry powder

1 Tbsp. mayonnaise

milk

To make pillows:

1 Preheat oven to 350 degrees.

2 In a large bowl, mix together cream cheese, green onion, mushrooms, 2 tablespoons butter, salt, and pepper.

3 Mix in chicken.

4 Open crescent rolls and separate each tube of dough into 4 rectangles. Press perforation in the center of each rectangle to seal and make a solid rectangle.

5 Spoon chicken mixture onto half of each rectangle. Divide chicken mixture evenly on each square of dough.

6 Fold over other half of crescent dough and press edges together to seal in mixture and make a pillow.

7 Dip each pillow in melted butter and roll them in the bread crumbs.

8 Place on baking sheet. Bake at 350 degrees for 15–20 minutes or until golden brown. Serve topped with cream sauce.

To make cream sauce:

1 Combine all cream sauce ingredients in a saucepan, using enough milk to make the consistency of a sauce or gravy. Cook over medium heat until heated thoroughly.

Serves 8.

Sour Cream Chili Bake

THIS YUMMY DISH IS ONE I MADE WHEN I WAS FIRST MARRIED AND HAVE BEEN
ENJOYING IT SINCE THEN.

1 lb. hamburger

¼ cup onion, chopped

1 (16-oz.) can red or kidney beans

1 (15-oz.) can chili

1 (15-oz.) can tomato sauce

1 pkg. taco seasoning

1 cup cheddar cheese, shredded

3½ cups Fritos® corn chips

1½ cups sour cream

1 Preheat oven to 350 degrees.

2 In a skillet, brown hamburger with onion; drain.

3 Stir in beans, chili, tomato sauce, taco seasoning, and ¼ cup cheese.

4 Sprinkle 2½ cups of Fritos® in bottom of a 9×13 baking dish.

5 Cover with meat mixture.

6 Bake uncovered for 20–25 minutes.

7 Spread sour cream over meat mixture.

8 Top with remaining Fritos® and cheese.

9 Bake uncovered for 3–5 minutes longer.

Serves 8–10.

Rice-A-Roni Casserole

I RECEIVED THIS RECIPE AS A GIFT WHEN I GOT MARRIED. IT'S ONE THAT I LOVE TO MAKE OFTEN AND IS ANOTHER FABULOUS 5-INGREDIENT RECIPE.

1 pkg. beef Rice-A-Roni®

1 lb. hamburger

1 medium onion, diced

1 (10¾-oz.) can condensed beef vegetable soup

1 can water

1 cup cheese, grated

1 Preheat oven to 350 degrees.

2 Cook Rice-A-Roni® according to package directions and set aside.

3 In a large skillet, brown hamburger with onion; drain.

4 Mix hamburger, Rice-A-Roni®, beef vegetable soup, and water together.

5 Place in a 9×13 dish and top with grated cheese.

6 Bake uncovered for 30 minutes until cheese melts and is hot.

Serves 4–6.

Mom's Oven Stew

THIS DELICIOUS STEW RECIPE COMES FROM MY MOTHER. THIS WAS A FAVORITE DISH OF MINE WHILE GROWING UP. IT'S ONE THAT I GET COMPLIMENTS ON EVERY TIME I MAKE IT.

1 onion, diced

2 cups potatoes, chunked

2 cups celery, chunked

2 cups carrots, chunked

1 (10¾-oz.) can tomato soup

1 (10¾-oz.) can cream of mushroom soup

1 can water

1 tsp. salt

½ tsp. pepper

1 Tbsp. sugar

2 Tbsp. rice, uncooked

1–1½ lbs. hamburger

1 Preheat oven to 325 degrees.

2 Chop vegetables and place in a roasting pan or 9×13 baking dish.

3 Combine soups, water, salt, pepper, sugar, and rice and mix well.

4 Pour soup mixture over vegetables.

5 Break up raw hamburger into chunks and sprinkle on top. The hamburger does not need to be browned.

6 Cover and bake for 3–5 hours, stirring occasionally. You may need to add a little water if it's too thick.

Serves 8.

Mom's Meatballs and Rice

THIS IS ANOTHER FAVORITE DISH OF MINE FROM MY MOM. I HAVE SEEN SIMILAR RECIPES REFERRED TO AS PORCUPINE MEATBALLS BECAUSE OF THE WAY THE RICE POKES OUT OF EACH MEATBALL.

1½ lbs. hamburger

¾ cup rice, uncooked

¾ cup evaporated milk

3 Tbsp. onion, chopped

1½ tsp. salt

⅛ tsp. pepper

1 (10¾-oz.) can condensed tomato soup

1¼ cups water

1 Preheat oven to 350 degrees.

2 In a medium bowl, combine hamburger, rice, evaporated milk, onion, salt, and pepper.

3 Shape into small balls (about 1½ inches in diameter).

4 In a skillet, brown meatballs; do not drain.

5 Transfer meatballs to a 9×13 pan.

6 Mix soup and water in the same pan used to cook meat.

7 Pour soup over meatballs.

8 Cover and bake at 350 degrees for 1½ hours.

Serves 6–8.

45-Minute Spaghetti

THIS IS ANOTHER FANTASTIC DISH COURTESY OF MY MOM. IT'S A FAMILY FAVORITE, EVEN FOR MY HUSBAND, WHO ISN'T A BIG SPAGHETTI FAN.

½ lb. hamburger

¾ cup onion, diced

¼ lb. bacon, cooked and diced

1 tsp. salt

⅛ tsp. pepper

2 tsp. sugar

2–3 dashes garlic powder or salt

1 tsp. Worcestershire sauce

1 cup water

1 (6-oz.) can tomato paste

1 (8-oz.) can tomato sauce

¼ cup olives, sliced (optional)

1 In a skillet, brown beef and onion together; drain.

2 Add remaining ingredients (except olives) to beef mixture.

3 Simmer, covered, for 20 minutes.

4 If desired, add sliced olives.

5 Cover and simmer for 15 minutes more.

6 Serve sauce over cooked spaghetti noodles.

Serves 6.

LAURA POWELL • 115

Popover Pizza

ANOTHER FAVORITE MEAL GROWING UP WAS POPOVER PIZZA. THIS WAS A RECIPE GIVEN TO MY MOTHER BY ONE OF HER DEAREST FRIENDS.

1½ lbs. meat (hamburger, sausage, ham, pepperoni, or whatever combination of meat you like)

1 medium onion, chopped

1 (28-oz. to 32-oz.) jar spaghetti sauce

3 cups mozzarella, shredded

2 eggs

1 cup milk

1 cup flour

1 Tbsp. cooking oil

½ tsp. salt

Parmesan cheese

1 Preheat oven to 400 degrees.

2 In a skillet, brown any meat that needs to be browned along with the onion; drain.

3 Combine spaghetti sauce with meat.

4 Pour meat mixture into a 9×13 pan.

5 Top with mozzarella cheese.

6 In a medium bowl, combine eggs, milk, flour, cooking oil, and salt.

7 Pour over cheese in pan.

8 Sprinkle with Parmesan cheese.

9 Bake uncovered for 35 minutes or until golden brown.

Serves 6–8.

Turkey-Cranberry Quesadillas

ONE OF MY FAVORITE WAYS TO USE UP LEFTOVER MEAT IS TO MAKE QUESADILLAS. THIS RECIPE IS PERFECT TO USE UP THOSE FABULOUS THANKSGIVING LEFTOVERS.

6   flour tortillas

2   Tbsp. butter, melted

Swiss cheese, shredded

green onion, diced

leftover turkey, diced or shredded

leftover cranberry sauce

1 Brush one side of the tortillas with melted butter.

2 Place tortilla butter side down in a frying pan.

3 Sprinkle half the tortilla with a layer of Swiss cheese and leftover turkey

4 Sprinkle on some green onion.

5 Spread cranberry sauce on the other half of the tortilla.

6 Cook over medium heat until under side is browned and crisp and cheese is melted.

7 Fold tortilla in half and remove from pan. Then cut in half so you have two triangles.

8 Repeat with remaining ingredients.

Serves 6.

Easy Breaded Chicken

I MADE THIS RECIPE AFTER LEARNING THE PROPER WAY TO BREAD CHICKEN FROM A
FRIEND WHO HAD WORKED AS A CHEF.

1 cup flour

2 eggs, beaten

¾ cup Panko bread crumbs

¾ cup (approximately) Italian
bread crumbs

salt and pepper to taste

6 chicken breasts

oil

1 Place flour on a plate and put beaten eggs in a
bowl.

2 Place bread crumbs in a bowl and mix with salt
and pepper to taste.

3 Start breading by coating chicken with flour.

4 Dip coated chicken breast in the egg followed
by the bread crumb mixture. Set aside and repeat
with remaining chicken breasts.

5 Cook the breaded chicken in a skillet coated
with oil until both sides are nice and brown and
the juices run clear.

Serves 6.

Cheesy Noodle Bake

THIS IS ONE OF MY FAVORITE GO-TO DINNER RECIPES. SO SIMPLE AND OH SO DELICIOUS!

2½ cups egg noodles

1 lb. hamburger

2 (8-oz.) cans tomato sauce

1 cup sour cream

1 cup cottage cheese

2 green onions, sliced

1 tsp. garlic salt

  cheese, shredded

1 Preheat oven to 350 degrees.

2 Cook egg noodles according to package and drain.

3 While noodles cook, brown hamburger until no longer pink; drain.

4 Mix tomato sauce into cooked hamburger.

5 Pour beef mixture into the bottom of a 7×11 or 2-quart baking dish.

6 Combine sour cream, cottage cheese, green onion, and garlic salt with the cooked noodles.

7 Pour noodle mixture in pan over beef mixture.

8 Top with shredded cheese.

9 Bake uncovered for 35–40 minutes until bubbly and cheese is melted.

Serves 6.

Hot Chicken and Rice Salad

I LOVE CHICKEN SALAD, AND THIS IS A YUMMY HOT VERSION. THIS CREAMY SALAD IS THE PERFECT COMFORT DISH. IT'S ALSO A GREAT WAY TO USE UP LEFTOVER RICE OR CHICKEN.

2 cups cooked chicken, diced

1 cup celery, diced

2 cups cooked rice

¾ cup mayonnaise

1 cup fresh mushrooms, sliced

1 tsp. lemon juice

   salt and pepper to taste

1 (10¾-oz.) can condensed cream of chicken soup

1 cup corn flakes

¼ cup butter, melted

1 (4-oz.) pkg. sliced almonds

1 Preheat oven to 400 degrees.

2 In a large bowl, mix together chicken, celery, rice, mayonnaise, mushrooms, lemon juice, salt, pepper, and cream of chicken soup until well combined.

3 Pour mixture into a sprayed 9×13 dish and spread out evenly in the dish.

4 Combine corn flakes with butter until corn flakes are well coated with butter.

5 Sprinkle corn flake mixture evenly over chicken/rice mixture.

6 Bake at 400 degrees, uncovered, for 15 minutes.

7 Remove dish from oven and sprinkle with sliced almonds.

8 Place dish back into oven for 5 more minutes.

Serves 6–8.

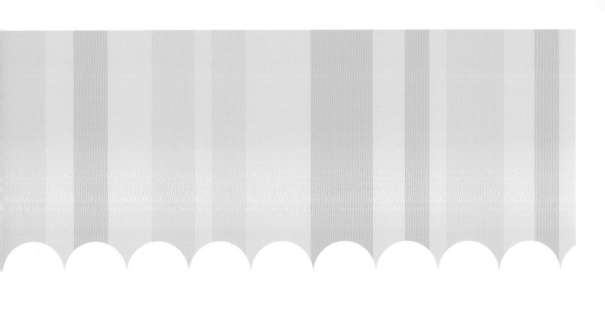

DESSERTS

Pastry Cream–Filled Filo Shells

THIS IS A QUICK DESSERT THAT LOOKS IMPRESSIVE. IT'S PERFECT FOR A TEA PARTY ON A SPRING AFTERNOON.

1 (5.1-oz.) pkg. instant chocolate pudding mix

½ cup milk

1½ cups heavy whipping cream

2 (1.9-oz.) pkgs. mini filo shells, thawed

fruit for garnish (such as mandarin oranges cut in half, raspberries, strawberry slices, banana slices, and so on)

1 In a large bowl, combine pudding mix, milk, and whipping cream.

2 Mix together by hand using a wire whisk. Mix well to ensure a smooth texture.

3 When the pudding starts to set, it is finished and needs to be used immediately.

4 Place filling into a large resealable bag or pastry bag. Squeeze out extra air and seal the top.

5 Pipe filling into each filo shell. (This filling will thicken as you chill the pastries.)

6 Garnish with fruit.

Makes 30 pastries.

White Texas Sheet Cake

I LOVE TEXAS SHEET CAKE, AND THIS WHITE VERSION IS A NICE CHANGE. PLUS, IT'S JUST AS YUMMY.

Cake:

1   cup butter

1   cup water

2   cups flour

2   cups sugar

2   eggs, beaten

½   cup sour cream

1   tsp. almond extract

1   tsp. baking soda

1   tsp. salt

Frosting:

½   cup butter

¼   cup milk

4½   cups confectioners' sugar

½   tsp. almond extract

To make cake:

1 Preheat oven to 375 degrees.

2 Grease a 15×10 jelly roll pan.

3 In a large saucepan, bring butter and water to a boil.

4 Remove saucepan from heat and add flour and sugar while still hot. Mix well.

5 Mix in eggs, sour cream, almond extract, baking soda, and salt. Do not mix too long.

6 Pour batter into the greased jelly roll pan.

7 Bake for 20 minutes or until a toothpick inserted into center of cake comes out clean.

To make frosting:

1 In a large saucepan, combine butter and milk and bring to a boil.

2 Remove from heat; stir in sugar and extract.

3 Spread over warm cake.

Serves 24.

Foamy Frosting

THIS IS MY FAVORITE HOMEMADE FROSTING RECIPE AND USUALLY WHAT WAS ON MY BIRTHDAY CAKES WHILE GROWING UP. I PREFER IT ON ANY KIND OF CHOCOLATE CAKE.

1   cup milk

5   Tbsp. flour

½   cup butter or margarine

½   cup shortening

1   cup sugar

1   tsp. vanilla

1   In a saucepan, cook milk and flour over medium heat until thick.

2   Remove from heat and allow to cool thoroughly.

3   In a bowl, cream together butter, shortening, and sugar.

4   Beat in cooled milk mixture until light and foamy.

5   Blend in vanilla.

Makes enough to frost a 9×13-inch cake.

Cake Mix Cookies

THIS IS A FUN RECIPE TO MAKE WITH YOUR KIDS. THESE COOKIES COME TOGETHER QUICKLY THANKS TO A CAKE MIX. PLUS THEY ARE SOFT AND DELICIOUS.

1 box cake mix (you choose the flavor—devil's food is our favorite)

2 eggs

⅓ cup oil

⅛–¼ cup water

any other ingredients you like

1 Preheat oven to 350 degrees.

2 Mix the cake mix, eggs, and oil.

3 Add enough water to make the mixture the consistency of cookie dough.

4 Mix in any other ingredients you like, such as dried fruit, chips, or nuts. (I use about 1½ cups peanut butter chips with the devil's food mix)

5 Drop dough by the spoonful on ungreased cookie sheet.

6 Bake at 350 degrees for 8–10 minutes until set in the middle.

Makes about 2 dozen cookies.

Cookie Sundaes

NOTHING BEATS A NICE WARM CHOCOLATE CHIP COOKIE—EXCEPT FOR ONE TOPPED WITH ICE CREAM AND HOT FUDGE.

1 stick butter, softened

1 egg

1 (17.5-oz.) pouch chocolate chip cookie mix or chocolate chip walnut mix

vanilla ice cream

chocolate syrup or hot fudge sauce

1 Preheat oven to 350 degrees.

2 Mix butter and egg in a bowl.

3 Then mix in cookie mix.

4 Put approximately ¼ cup of the cookie mix in a greased 6-oz. ramekin. Flatten out dough. You should get enough for 7 ramekins from 1 mix.

5 Bake for 18–22 minutes. The center needs to be even with the rest of the cookie and not look wet. You can also test with a toothpick.

6 Allow cookies to cool in the ramekin for 1 minute and then invert onto a dish.

7 Now give the cookie a little time to cool. You want it warm, but not warm enough to completely melt the ice cream (wait about 8 minutes).

8 Top with ice cream and sauce.

Serves 7.

Marshmallow Brownies

I LOVE A GOOD BROWNIE, BUT BROWNIES TOPPED WITH MARSHMALLOWS AND FROSTING ARE EVEN BETTER!

Brownies:

1 (18.3-oz.) box fudge brownie mix, prepared and baked according to package directions for cakelike brownies

miniature marshmallows

Frosting:

½ cup butter

4 Tbsp. unsweetened cocoa powder

3 Tbsp. water

3 Tbsp. milk

3½ cups confectioners' sugar

1 tsp. vanilla extract

To make brownies:

1 When brownies are done, cover them with a layer of miniature marshmallows and put back into oven for a few minutes until marshmallows are nice and puffy.

2 Cool brownies and top with frosting recipe below.

To make frosting:

1 In a medium saucepan, bring butter or margarine, cocoa, water, and milk to a boil.

2 Remove from heat.

3 While cocoa mixture is still hot, add confectioners' sugar and vanilla.

4 Beat well.

5 Pour frosting over brownies while frosting is still hot.

6 Allow to cool. Cut with a plastic knife so the marshmallows won't stick to it.

Serves 12.

Over-the-Top Peanut Butter Cookies

WHY SETTLE FOR REGULAR PEANUT BUTTER COOKIES WHEN YOU CAN HAVE AN OVER-THE-TOP PEANUT BUTTER COOKIE TOPPED WITH PEANUT BUTTER AND CHOCOLATE CANDY? THIS IS A GREAT WAY TO USE UP LEFTOVER HALLOWEEN CANDY.

¾ cup butter, softened

1 cup sugar

1 cup brown sugar

1 cup peanut butter

2 large eggs

2 tsp. vanilla

1 tsp. baking soda

½ tsp. salt

2½ cups flour

1½ cups milk chocolate chips

36 mini Reese's® peanut butter cups, each cut into 4 pieces

1 Preheat oven to 350 degrees.

2 In a large bowl, mix softened butter, sugar, brown sugar, peanut butter, eggs, and vanilla.

3 Add soda, salt, and flour.

4 Fold in chocolate chips.

5 Using an ice cream scoop, place 6 scoops of dough on an ungreased cookie sheet. (These are **big** cookies.)

6 Use your hand and slightly flatten each scoop of dough.

7 Bake each batch for 12 minutes.

8 Remove cookies from oven and lightly press 8 cut-up pieces of Reese's® peanut butter cups over the top of each cookie.

9 Return cookies to oven for 2 more minutes.

10 Cool on baking sheet for 2 minutes before placing on cooling rack.

Makes 18 cookies. These cookies are best if eaten the same day.

Pumpkin Chocolate Chip Cookies

PUMPKIN CHOCOLATE CHIP COOKIES ARE A CLASSIC. WITH THIS RECIPE, YOU CAN STICK WITH A CLASSIC OR CHANGE IT UP WITH CINNAMON CHIPS.

½ cup shortening

1½ cups sugar

1 egg

1 cup pumpkin

2½ cups flour

1 tsp. baking powder

1 tsp. baking soda

½ tsp. salt

1 tsp. vanilla

1 tsp. nutmeg

1 tsp. cinnamon

1 (12-oz.) bag chocolate chips

1 Preheat oven to 400 degrees.

2 In a bowl, cream shortening and sugar together.

3 Mix in egg and pumpkin.

4 Add remaining ingredients.

5 Drop dough by spoonfuls on greased cookie sheet.

6 Bake for 10 minutes.

Makes about 2–3 dozen.

Microwave Caramel Popcorn

I LOVE TO SNACK ON CARAMEL POPCORN. THIS MICROWAVE VERSION IS PERFECT FOR WHENEVER I GET A CRAVING. I DO ONLY 2 QUARTS OF POPCORN BECAUSE I LIKE MY POPCORN WELL COATED.

½ cup butter

1 cup brown sugar

¼ cup light corn syrup

½ tsp. salt

¾ tsp. baking soda

2–3 quarts popped popcorn

1 In a large, microwave-safe bowl, microwave butter, brown sugar, corn syrup, and salt on high for 2½ to 3 minutes until bubbling.

2 Remove from microwave and mix in baking soda.

3 Put popped popcorn in a paper grocery sack and pour caramel over popcorn.

4 Fold down top of grocery sack and put in the microwave.

5 Microwave on high for 1 minute and 20 seconds.

6 Take sack out of microwave and shake to evenly coat the popcorn.

7 Pour out on cookie sheet to cool.

Makes 2–3 quarts.

Make You Cry Mint Chocolate Ice Cream Pie

THIS WAS A RECIPE I CREATED ONE YEAR FOR MY HUSBAND ON FATHER'S DAY. MINT CHOCOLATE CHIP ICE CREAM IS ONE OF HIS FAVORITE TREATS!

Pie:

- 4 cups mint chocolate chip ice cream
- 1 prepared Oreo® cookie pie crust
- 5 Oreo® cookies, coarsely crushed

  chocolate sauce (recipe below)

  sweetened whipped cream

Chocolate Sauce:

- ½ cup sugar
- 3 oz. evaporated milk or cream
- 3 Tbsp. cocoa
- 1 Tbsp. butter
- 1 tsp. vanilla

To make pie:

1 Let the ice cream sit out for a little bit to soften.

2 Once softened, scoop ice cream into the pie crust and spread evenly.

3 Top with crushed Oreo® cookies.

4 Top with the prepared chocolate sauce.

5 Cover and place in your freezer.

6 Remove from freezer 10 minutes before serving and top each serving with sweetened whipped cream.

To make chocolate sauce:

1 Mix all ingredients in a saucepan.

2 Cook over medium heat and bring to a boil.

3 Boil for 1 minute and remove from heat.

4 Allow to cool. You will have a little more than you need for the pie (about ¼–⅓ cup), but just save it and use it for a bowl of ice cream another day.

Serves 6–8.

Grandma's Hot Fudge Sauce

GRANDMA ALWAYS MADE THIS YUMMY SAUCE TO SERVE OVER HOMEMADE ICE CREAM.

4 Tbsp. cocoa powder

2 cups sugar

4 Tbsp. flour

   dash of salt

1 (12-oz.) can evaporated milk

1 In a saucepan, combine cocoa powder, sugar, flour, and salt.

2 Whisk together until well blended.

3 Whisk in evaporated milk and bring to a boil over medium heat.

4 Remove from heat and cool slightly.

5 Serve over ice cream.

Makes about 2 cups.

Turtle Cake

THIS CAKE IS OOEY GOOEY AND OH SO DELICIOUS. NOT A FAN OF NUTS? NO PROBLEM! JUST OMIT THEM FROM THE RECIPE.

1 box German chocolate cake mix

¾ cup butter, melted

1 (14-oz.) bag caramels, unwrapped

½ cup evaporated milk

2 cups pecans, chopped (optional)

1 cup chocolate chips

1 Preheat oven to 350 degrees.

2 Prepare cake mix according to package directions.

3 Place half of the cake batter into a well-greased 9×13 pan.

4 Bake at 350 degrees for 15 minutes.

5 Meanwhile, combine butter, caramels, and milk in a saucepan.

6 Cook over low heat, stirring constantly, until caramels are melted and mixture is creamy.

7 Pour caramel mixture over partially cooked cake.

8 Then sprinkle 1 cup of pecans and all the chocolate chips over the caramel mixture and cake.

9 Pour remaining cake batter over nuts and chocolate chips.

10 Sprinkle remaining pecans over batter.

11 Bake at 350 degrees for 25 minutes.

Serves 12–15.

Chocolate Chip Paradise Sundae

THIS RECIPE MAKES ENOUGH TO SERVE A LARGE GROUP. THE COOKIE BASE IS ALSO WONDERFUL TO EAT WITHOUT THE ICE CREAM AND TOPPINGS.

3 cups brown sugar, firmly packed

1½ cups butter, melted

6 eggs

3 tsp. vanilla

3 cups flour

1 tsp. baking powder

1 cup walnuts, chopped

1 cup coconut

2 cups milk chocolate chips

vanilla ice cream

caramel sauce

hot fudge sauce

walnuts, chopped

1 Preheat oven to 325 degrees.

2 Grease a 12×17 jelly roll pan.

3 In a large bowl, combine sugar and melted butter.

4 Beat with electric mixer.

5 Add eggs, one at a time, along with vanilla, and mix well.

6 In another bowl, whisk flour and baking powder together.

7 Add flour/baking powder mixture to sugar/butter mixture and blend until combined.

8 Fold in walnuts, coconut, and chocolate chips.

9 Pour into a greased jelly roll pan.

10 Bake for 40 minutes until a toothpick inserted in the center comes out clean.

11 Cut into 24 squares. Serve warm or reheat individual servings in the microwave (10 seconds for a serving).

12 Top each serving with a scoop of ice cream. Then drizzle with caramel sauce and hot fudge sauce.

13 Sprinkle with chopped walnuts.

Serves 24.

Punch Bowl Trifle

THIS IS ANOTHER GREAT RECIPE TO SERVE FOR A LARGE CROWD. DON'T HAVE A CROWD? THEN FREEZE HALF THE CAKE AND USE A SMALLER BOX OF PUDDING TO HALF THE RECIPE.

1 box yellow cake mix, prepared and baked

3 large bananas, sliced and soaked in reserved pineapple juice

1 (5.1-oz.) pkg. instant vanilla pudding mix, prepared according to package directions

1 (20-oz.) can pineapple tidbits, drained and juice reserved

1 (21-oz.) can cherry pie filling

1 (12-oz.) container whipped topping

1 Allow cake to cool, then cut cake with a serrated knife into small, bite-sized squares.

2 Place half of the cake pieces into the bottom of a large punch bowl.

3 Drain bananas from pineapple juice.

4 Next, layer half of each ingredient on top of the cake in this order: pudding, pineapple, bananas, cherry pie filling, whipped topping.

5 Place remaining cake pieces on top of whipped topping and repeat layers.

6 Chill for at least 2 hours before serving.

Serves 12–16.

Lemon Cream Cheese Pie

TANGY LEMON PUDDING PAIRS WELL WITH A SOFT CREAM CHEESE LAYER IN THIS PIE.

1¼   cups cold milk

1   (3.3-oz.) pkg. instant lemon pudding mix

1   (8-oz.) pkg. cream cheese

¾   cup powdered sugar

1   (8-oz.) container whipped topping

1   prepared shortbread pie crust

1 In a bowl, beat milk and lemon pudding mix with hand mixer for 2 minutes. Set mixture aside.

2 In another bowl, whip together cream cheese, powdered sugar, and ⅓ cup whipped topping.

3 Beat until well combined.

4 Spread cream cheese mixture into the bottom of the pie crust.

5 Pour pudding mixture over cream cheese layer.

6 Place in the refrigerator for at least 1 hour.

7 Before serving, top pie with remaining whipped topping.

Serves 6–8.

Pumpkin Bars

THESE PUMPKIN BARS CAN BE TOPPED WITH CHOCOLATE CHIPS OR SWEET CREAM CHEESE FROSTING. I LIKE TO DO HALF AND HALF.

6 eggs

1½ cups canola oil

3 cups sugar

1½ tsp. vanilla

1 large (29-oz.) can pumpkin

3¼ cups flour

1½ tsp. baking soda

1 Tbsp. cinnamon

1½ tsp. salt

2 cups chocolate chips
or cream cheese frosting
(see next page)

1 Preheat oven to 350 degrees.

2 Mix together eggs, oil, sugar, vanilla, and pumpkin.

3 Fold in dry ingredients and pour into a 12×17 jelly roll pan. If using chocolate chips, sprinkle batter with chocolate chips.

4 Bake for 30–40 minutes until a toothpick inserted in the center comes out clean. Do not overbake.

5 If not using chocolate chips, frost with cream cheese frosting (see recipe on following page).

Serves 24–30.

Cream Cheese Frosting

2 (8-oz.) pkgs. cream cheese, softened

1 cup butter, softened

2 cups powdered sugar

2 tsp. vanilla

1 In a medium bowl, blend together cream cheese and butter until smooth.

2 Beat in powdered sugar and vanilla.

Makes 3 cups.

Cereal Candy

THIS RECIPE IS ONE I MAKE EACH YEAR AT CHRISTMASTIME. IT IS DELICIOUS AND HIGHLY ADDICTIVE. MY FAMILY COULD FINISH OFF A WHOLE RECIPE IN ONE EVENING IF I LET THEM.

5 cups Cheerios®

5 cups Rice Chex®

6 cups Special K™

2 cups sugar

¾ cup white corn syrup

½ cup butter (no substitutes)

dash of salt

1 cup whipping cream

1 tsp. vanilla

1 In a large bowl, combine all cereals.

2 In a large saucepan, combine sugar, corn syrup, butter, and dash of salt over medium heat.

3 Bring to a boil, stirring constantly.

4 When boiling, slowly stir in whipping cream.

5 Using a candy thermometer, cook to soft ball stage while stirring constantly.

6 Once at soft ball stage, remove from heat immediately and stir in vanilla.

7 Pour over your cereal. Then gently toss and coat the cereal.

8 Once all cereal is coated, pour out on a large cookie sheet to cool.

Serves 16.

Brownies for a Crowd

THIS RECIPE MAKES ENOUGH TO FEED A CROWD AND IS EXCELLENT FOR BAKE SALES AND GET-TOGETHERS.

Brownies:

8 eggs

4 cups sugar

2 tsp. salt

4 tsp. vanilla

2 cups butter, melted

3 cups flour

1½ cups cocoa

Frosting:

4 cups powdered sugar

½ cup butter, softened

½ cup cocoa

milk

To make brownies:

1 Preheat oven to 350 degrees.

2 In a large bowl, beat eggs with a mixer until well blended.

3 Add sugar, salt, and vanilla and beat for 1 minute.

4 Then add melted butter, a little at a time, while blending.

5 In another bowl, mix flour and cocoa with a whisk until well blended.

6 Add flour/cocoa mixture to egg mixture and mix until well combined.

7 Spread onto a greased 12×17 jelly roll pan.

8 Bake for 20–25 minutes.

9 Cool for 15 minutes and spread with frosting.

To make frosting:

1 In a large bowl, blend powdered sugar, butter, and cocoa along with enough milk to make the frosting a spreadable consistency.

2 Spread over the brownies after they have cooled for 15 minutes.

3 Keep spreading because the frosting melts, making it nice and even on the brownies. Allow brownies to continue to cool.

Serves 30.

Éclairs

WHEN I WAS GROWING UP, MY MOM WOULD OCCASIONALLY TAKE US TO THE BAKERY AS A TREAT. WHENEVER POSSIBLE, I WOULD GET AN ÉCLAIR. NOW I CAN MAKE THEM AT HOME!

Pastry:

1 cup water

½ cup butter

¼ tsp. salt

1 cup flour

4 eggs

To make pastry:

1 Preheat oven to 400 degrees.

2 In a large saucepan, bring water, butter, and salt to a boil over medium heat.

3 Add flour all at once.

4 Stir until a smooth ball forms.

5 Remove from heat; let stand for 5 minutes.

6 Add eggs, one at a time, beating well after each addition. Beat until smooth and shiny.

7 Insert a ¾-inch round tip into a pastry bag or heavy-duty resealable plastic bag and add the batter to the bag.

8 Pipe into strips about 3½ inches long, spacing about 3 inches apart on a greased baking sheet.

9 Bake at 400 degrees for 30–35 minutes or until golden brown.

10 Remove and place on a wire rack.

11 Poke a hole in one end of each pastry with a straw or chopstick. This hole will be used to add the filling.

12 Allow to cool.

Makes 24 pastries.

Filling:

1 (5.1-oz.) pkg. instant vanilla pudding mix

2 cups heavy whipping cream

Chocolate Glaze:

4 squares semisweet chocolate or 4 oz. semisweet chips

3 Tbsp. butter

1½ cups powdered sugar

3 Tbsp. hot water

To make filling:

1 In a large bowl, combine pudding and whipping cream. Mix together well by hand using a wire whisk to ensure a smooth texture. When the pudding starts to set, the filling is finished and needs to be used immediately.

2 Place filling into a large resealable bag or pastry bag. Squeeze out extra air and seal the top. If using resealable bag, cut a hole in one corner of the bag small enough to fit into the hole in the pastry.

3 Pipe filling into each pastry shell. (This filling will thicken as you chill the pastries.)

To make chocolate glaze:

1 Place chocolate and butter in a 1-quart microwave-safe dish and cook on high for 1–1½ minutes, stirring every 30 seconds until smooth.

2 Whisk in powdered sugar and hot water until mixture is smooth.

3 Spread glaze on top of each pastry.

4 Refrigerate pastries at least 1 hour.

Makes enough for 24 pastries.

Index

About the Author

Laura Powell grew up in the Salt Lake Valley. She gained a passion for cooking from her mother, created her own recipe book as a young girl, and participated in a summer cooking program through the *Deseret News*. She began her blog, RealMomKitchen.com, in April 2008 as a way to showcase her passion for cooking. Since then RealMomKitchen.com has turned into her own small business. Laura resides in Utah with her husband and three children.